Temple Beth David
6100 Hefley Street
Westminster, CA 92683
(714) 892-6623

A Dictionary of
Jewish Names
and their History

BENZION C. KAGANOFF

To Hans & Ellen Goldsmith with best wishes & regards —

SCHOCKEN BOOKS • NEW YORK

First published by SCHOCKEN BOOKS 1977

10 9 8 7 6 5   85 86 87 88

Copyright © 1977 by Schocken Books Inc.

Library of Congress Cataloging in Publication Data

Kaganoff, Benzion C.
  A dictionary of Jewish names and their history.

  Bibliography: p. 212
  Includes indexes.
  1. Names, Personal—Jewish. I. Title.
CS3010.k28   929.4′02′4296   77-70277

Manufactured in the United States of America
ISBN 0–8052–3660–0 (hardcover)
     0–8052–0643–4 (paperback)

NOTE TO READER: A consistent system of spelling and transliteration proved impossible for many words and names that have been refracted through various languages in their long history. The goal, therefore, was to maintain clarity rather than consistency. The reader should see the note on pages 123–124 for some further explanation of the problems of transliteration.

To Claire (Chaya):

With a prayer—

"Grow old along with me!
The best is yet to be."

Preface

It is now one hundred and forty years since Leopold Zunz, one of the founders of the Science of Judaism *(Wissenschaft des Judentums)*, wrote his treatise *Die Namen der Juden (The Names of the Jews)*, the first study of Jewish family and first names.

What is quite remarkable is that in the course of the five generations since Zunz, except for an article here and there, no book has ever been published in the English language on this subject. In fact, even articles in English are few and far between, and very little has been published since the appearance of my two articles in the 1950s (see Bibliography). The present volume will, I hope, fill a long-felt need in the field of Jewish onomastics.

The search for a suitable name for our three daughters—Aleta, Yarona (Roni), and Penny—was the motivation that proved to be, for me, the beginning of a fascinating journey through the wonderland of Jewish history, etymology, linguistics, and folkore. I am still searching and continue to be amazed and delighted at new surprises that I discover. The investigation of a Jewish family name is charged with all the suspense of a thrilling detective story.

I wish to express my deepest appreciation to the staff

members of the American Jewish Historical Society Library and Archives in Waltham, Massachusetts, the Asher Library of the Spertus College of Judaica in Chicago, and the Saul Silber Memorial Library of the Hebrew Theological College in Skokie, Illinois, for making available to me books, periodicals, and other materials that I needed for my research. Their cooperation has been most gracious and wholehearted.

My sincere thanks to Mrs. David (Geri) Jankelovitz for her work in the technical preparation of typing the manuscript and index.

I regret very much that, because of space limitations, the history and derivation of many more names could not be included, but part of the responsibility of an author is "to make a long story short."

I have been most fortunate in serving for more than two decades as Rabbi of Congregation Ezras Israel. I am especially grateful for the many opportunities to study, to teach, and to grow which have been afforded to me.

Finally, I am thankful for the tradition of learning and the love of Israel which I have received from my revered father, Rabbi David Kaganoff of blessed memory, and my dear mother, Miriam Kaganoff—a tradition that I hope will be cherished and perpetuated by our children.

There are no words to adequately express my gratitude to my dear wife, Claire, and to our children for their love, encouragement, and devotion.

BENZION C. KAGANOFF

Chicago, Illinois
Passover 5737
April 7, 1977

Contents

of Angels/Names of Animals/Names Determine Destiny/Only Hebrew Is Spoken in Heaven/Who Selects a Name?/When Is the Child Named?

Part II
A Dictionary of Selected Jewish Names

Introduction

WE HAVE REACHED a point in American Jewish history when—certainly with regard to information about our family and personal names—one can no longer follow the Biblical directive: "Ask your father and he will declare to you, your elders and they will tell you."

In preparation for this book, I conducted an informal survey among my colleagues in the Orthodox rabbinate. Two interesting facts came to light. In the first place, I became aware of the extent of Americanization that had taken place even within that bulwark of tradition. Quite a number began their responses with an explanation that the name which they bear is not really the original name but had undergone various modifications and transformations that we are accustomed to find among so many Jewish names today.

Secondly, it came somewhat as a surprise to discover how uninformed and misinformed so many were about the meaning and origin of their family names. Many indicated that they had sought information from parents or grandparents but could not be enlightened.

All this should really come as no surprise. The bridge between the Old World and America has become weaker and weaker with each passing generation. Recent demographic studies indicate that about 75 per cent to 80 per cent of the American Jewish population is native born. This means that only about one-fourth to one-fifth of all the Jews in the United States is foreign born, and this percentage represents, for the most part, the older population. This is the average. In many suburban communities, the Jewish population is almost totally native born.

These statistics are one of many indicators pointing to the fact that American Jewry has become thoroughly Americanized. This process of acculturation has been going on for a long time. With this process has come a remarkable leveling. Democracy equalizes; it tends to bring about a uniformity of language, mores, customs, and personal and family names. A Kohen, a Kovacs, a Kowalsky, and a Koronakis emerge as an ambiguous Cole or amorphous Kay in the American melting pot, and the Jewish, Hungarian, Polish, and Greek origins dissipate in the American experience.

Some will call this normal adjustment and accept it as the inevitable process of a minority's response to a majority culture and environment. Others may decry this as creeping assimilation or worse. One fact is clear. Even the most religiously motivated and identity-conscious Jews have become acculturated—as far as their names are concerned.

And yet, while we may be able to do very little to stop this process, we would lose a great deal if we did not attempt to record and salvage something of a vanishing past. And that is the purpose of this book. Goethe was certainly right when he reminded us that "a man's name is not like a cloak that merely hangs about him and that one may safely twitch and pull, but a perfectly fitting garment that, like the skin, envelops him so tightly one cannot scratch or scrape it without injuring the man himself."

This book will try to discover what there is behind each Jewish personal and family name. It will attempt to trace the historical processes that created the name forms that appear today. Etymology and philology reveal to us the word root or stem from which a name is derived, and what appears to be its meaning. Onomastics, the study of names, goes beyond origin and meaning—it takes into account transmutations, usage, naming traditions, and all kinds of subtle nuances that lie beneath the meaning and form of a personal or family name.

My own interest in this subject spans almost a quarter of a century. Over the years I have collected a treasure of data on Jewish names. I have had the opportunity to answer many inquiries regarding names, both by letter and from the lecture platform. My two articles published in *Commentary* more than two decades ago have remained standard reference works on the subject, and I am deeply grateful to the American Jewish Committee for permission to incorporate material from these articles into this book.

PART I

A HISTORY
OF JEWISH NAMES

1

In the Beginning

THE LONGEST JEWISH family name is Katzenellenbogen. It was assumed by Meir ben Isaac who was born about 1480 and died in 1565. Renowned among Talmudic scholars as the chief rabbi of the Venetian Republic, he derived his family name from the locality of Katzenelnbogen, the place of his birth in the Prussian province of Hesse-Nassau.

Popular etymology associated Katzenellenbogen with the two German words which mean, literally, "the cat's elbow." But the name has little association with cats and even less with elbows. It comes from an old geographic name, Cattimelibochi, for a part of Hesse that combines several ancient Germanic tribes that first settled there. The name of one of these tribes, the Chatti, is recognizable in the first element of the name.

Katzenellenbogen is an old, widely ramified family whose various branches spread to Italy, Poland, Germany, Alsace, and America. Variants of the original name appear in the form of Ellbogen, Ellenbogen, Bogen, Katzenelson, Katzin, and Ellen. There is even a Hebraized version: *katzin*, that is, "chief" Elin Bogen.

A remarkable legend is associated with the life of Saul Katzenellenbogen, grandson of Meir. Saul is said to have been chosen king of Poland for one day in 1586. While the story has no historical basis, it caught the imagination of medieval Jewry and was passed on from generation to generation with all kinds of variations. Although he was never elected king of Poland, Saul was a real person, and the myth caused him to be known as Saul Wahl (*Wahl* in German [and Yiddish] means "choice," or "election," a reminder of the legend), which many of his descendants adopted as their family name. However, in Poland, where Saul lived and died, the German name, Wahl, was understood as the Polish word *wol* ("ox"). From this various branches of the family transformed the name into Ochs, Byk, and Schorr—all of which mean "ox" or "bull" in German, Polish, and Hebrew, respectively.

Or take the family name Atlas. There are several possible origins for that name. It may be derived from the word *Atlas*, which means "satin" in German. The individual who first assumed the name may have been a manufacturer or seller of satin. But the name may also be a matronymic, signifying one who is descended from a woman by the name of Edel (or Adele or Ethel, which mean "noble"). The name was Edels and became Atlas. It was not unusual for Jews to pay tribute to a matriarch by selecting a family name in her honor. Often, the wife or mother-in-law was the family's breadwinner, while the husband or son-in-law continued to study in a *yeshivah*.

Finally, the name Atlas may be an acrostic for a*kh* to*v* le*yisrael selah*, "Truly, God is good to Israel" (Psalm 73:1). The bearer of the name selected the Biblical verse in praise of the Almighty and as a prayer of hope for the future.

Some names have one meaning when found among non-Jews and a completely different meaning when used by Jews. As a German name Krieger or Kriegman means "warrior." As a Jewish name it indicates a tavern-keeper, the owner of an inn with a sign of a pitcher or jug—*Krug* (also pronounced *krig* in Yiddish)—on the outside.

Kessler as a non-Jewish family name refers to a coppersmith, more specifically to a boilermaker or one who made or sold kettles. But Jewish Kesslers derive their name not from a profession but from the Hebrew name of an ancestor called Yekutiel (Yekusiel), whose nickname was Kessel. Kessler means "one descended from Kessel."

The English name Cooper signified a maker or seller of barrels, casks, and tubs. Cooperman is the cooper's helper or servant. As a Jewish name Cooper and Cooperman is derived from the German *Kupfer* ("copper") and means "coppersmith."

In the same way, Schoen as a non-Jewish name refers to the bearer as a handsome beautiful person (from German *schoen*); as a Jewish name it is an abbreviation of sh*aliah* n*eeman,* the trusted representative of the community.

Schatz is the German word for "treasure" and Schatzmann means "treasurer." As a Jewish family name it stands for sh*aliah* tz*ibbur,* the leader of prayers in the synagogue—a name often assumed by the cantor.

The above examples have been selected to illustrate that there is a great deal more behind a Jewish family name than the appearance of the word. Some Jewish family names, of course, are quite easy to trace. For example, a name found among Sephardic Jews—Moshiah (Messiah)—originally signified a zealous follower of Sabbatai Tzevi, the false messiah who very nearly succeeded in imposing himself on Israel in the seventeenth century. Similarly, Cohen and Levy are direct transliterations of Hebrew words that make it clear that the one is a man of priestly lineage and the other a Jew of Levitic extraction.

But in general, family names are infinitely more varied than personal names, having been culled from more diverse sources, having undergone more changes of form, and having come from many more different languages. Family names, or surnames, are not, in any case, as "standardized" as personal names or first names. We feel freer to touch them up, trim them, or change them altogether. This is why the origins of many names are lost.

Even where a name survives in its original form we may have trouble—as with those which derive from abbreviations whose meaning was once clear but which cannot now be deciphered with certainty. To cite some examples: Charlap can either be an abbreviation of h*asan reb Layb Pinhas*, "the son-in-law of Layb Pinhas," or of anyone whose names began with the letters "l" and "p." Who that someone was, we no longer know; but at the time the name was assumed, he was so well known that his son-in-law basked in his glory. But Charlap can also stand for h*arif limdinat polin*, "the brilliant scholar of the country of Poland"—a name that originated with a distinguished dynasty of rabbinic scholars. A scion of the Charlap family recently advised the author that, according to a family tradition, the name is an abbreviation of *Chiya rosh legalut polin*, "Chiya, head of the Polish diaspora." It could also stand for *Chiya rosh liglil polin*, "Chiya, head of the region of Poland."

The name Shulvass (or Schulweis, as some members of the family spell it) appears at first glance to have some association with a "white synagogue" (which is its literal meaning). One might assume that the original bearer of the name was a synagogue functionary. Actually, the word Shulvass represents an acrostic for the phrase sh*e-ezke lirot binhomat tzion*, "May I be worthy to see Zion consoled" (sh-l-b-s). This phrase was used as a closing in letter writing. Hebrew, of course, is written without the vowels shown; and *b* and *v* are the same letter in Hebrew. One also discovers, by means of this name, that at the time the name was assumed the Hebrew letter *tzaddi* was pronounced more like the sound *s* and not with the sound *tz* as is the case now.

In order to understand the entire panorama of Jewish family names, we must go back to the very origin of our people. At the beginning of the Biblical period, Jews, like all members of ancient societies, had no surnames. Men were known simply as Abraham, Isaac, Jacob, Moses, and so forth. But as the patriarchal families swelled into tribes, more definite identifications were deemed necessary, and patronymics began to be used: a man was designated as "X" *ben* ("son of") "Y." Thus we find: Joshua *ben* Nun, Caleb *ben* Yefuneh, Palti *ben* Raphu, and so on. The patronymic is the form of many surnames extant today, both among Jews and non-Jews: Jameson, Johnson, Jackson, Abramson.

In the later period covered by the books of Judges and Kings we find places of origin being employed to identify individuals: Doeg the Edomite, Uriah the Hittite, Elijah the Tishbite, etc. At the time of the return from the exile in Babylon under Ezra we come upon several descriptive and adjectival personal names with a definite article. These, to be sure, occur only rarely, but they supply interesting examples of personal names that at the same time serve very nearly as surnames: *Hakotz* ("the thorn") in Ezra 2:61; *Hakatan* ("the little one") in Ezra 8:12; *Halohesh* ("the enchanter") in Nehemiah 3:12. This sort of name probably constitutes the transition to the more definite types of surnames that make their appearance in the Talmudic period.

The Biblical style of nomenclature persisted through Talmudic times, but with several innovations. Patronymics are quite prevalent in the Talmud; Johanan ben Zakkai, Joshua ben Hananiah, Simon ben Gamliel. But since some individuals bore the same personal and patronymic names, it was occasionally necessary to base a surname on other family relationships. Thus we get Rabba bar bar Hana (Rabba the grandson of Hana), Levi the son-in-law of Zechariah, Hama the father of Hoshaiah, Tahlifa the father-in-law of Abbahu, and so on.

Places of origin continued to be used as surnames in Talmudic times: Nahum the Mede, Nahum of Gimso, Todos of Rome, Levites of Yabneh, Hillel the Babylonian, Jose the

Galilean. Iscariot (Judas) and Magdalene (Mary) in the New Testament are also place names, the former being Judas *ish* Kriot, "Judas the man of Kriot"; the latter, Miriam of Magdela.

Priestly designations are first used for surnames in the Talmudic era: Ishmael the High Priest; Jose Hakohen (Jose the Priest); Hanina the Chief of the Priests *(segan hakohanim)*. At least one surname of the period came from a position within a family: Tabot Rishba, which signifies "chief of the family."

Men also earned surnames: Samuel the Astronomer; Hanina Kara (Hanina the Bible Teacher); Hutzpith the Interpreter, or Translator *(hameturgeman)*; Ephraim Safra (Ephraim the Scribe), and so on. In the crafts we find: Johanan the Sandalmaker; Daniel the Tailor; Ada the Waiter; Isaac the Smith. We are familiar with occupational surnames today, both among Jews and non-Jews: thus Smith, Taylor, and Schneider ("tailor," in German); Carpenter, Becker (Baker), Shoemaker.

Nicknames also make their first appearance as a source of surnames in the Talmudic period: Hillel the Old Man; Zeira the Younger; Abba Arekha (Abba the Tall); Samuel Hakatan (Samuel the Short); Jose Katanta (Jose the Little One). The Talmud mentions a Tayfa, as well as an Isaac, Sammoka (the Red), called so because of the color of their hair or complexions.

None of those surnames, however, had the major characteristic of modern family names; transmissibility from one generation to another. They remained attached to the individual and were not inherited by his descendants. Of all ancient names, those of kings and priests approached the notion of inherited family names most closely. The royal dynasty was called Beth David (House of David); the priestly class was Beth Aaron (House of Aaron). During the Second Commonwealth, when the Davidic line had for all practical purposes disappeared politically, family names began to be perpetuated among the priesthood, where the practice caught on because of the various functions in the Temple that were the special province of certain families. The Talmud (Tractate Yoma) mentions a priestly family, Beth Abtinas (House of Abtinas), that monopolized the secret of preparing the frankincense used in the Temple; we also hear of Beth Garmo, which alone possessed the secret of baking the shewbread.

Another indication that priestly family names were transmitted is the case of the Hasmoneans, in whom the sole political leadership of Judea was vested for many generations. According to Josephus, "Hasmonean" was derived from Hasmoneus, the great-grandfather of Mattathias, and was borne by all his descendants. And so while each of the five sons of Mattathias had his own particular surname (the most famous being that of Judah, which was Maccabeus), the name Hasmonean was inherited by all members of the line.

There were no further changes in the ways of selecting surnames for a long time after the destruction of the Second Temple in 70 C.E. In this respect the Jews remained uninfluenced by the Romans who, among all the ancient people, had the most highly developed system of personal nomenclature. It was only in the tenth and eleventh centuries that family names began to become common, among Jews and non-Jews both.

2

From JOHN doe to john DOE

EXACTLY WHEN THE FIRST hereditary family names originated is impossible to say. Nor did family names develop all at once. As a matter of fact, family names followed varying patterns among different peoples and cultures.

Chinese society has had the institution of hereditary family names since the fourth pre-Christian century. Family names may have developed among the Hindus even earlier.

In the Western world, the Romans had the most sophisticated and highly developed system of nomenclature. This system of naming was used during the entire republican epoch and later in the empire. Toward the end of the empire, however, the naming pattern began to change and subsequently was lost. One reason was that people used names that did not indicate a family tie. A slave would select the name of the master who set him free, and the number of freed slaves continued to grow and grow. Also, anyone who was granted Roman citizenship acquired the name of the magistrate who made the decision. Thus in 212 C.E. all free inhabitants of the Roman Empire were given citizenship by the emperor Caracalla, with the result that hundreds of thousands of Greeks, Syrians, Africans, etc., adopted the emperor's name. In this way, time-honored Roman names lost their significance.

Another influence was introduced by the Christians, who very often belonged to the lower social classes and were not especially concerned with the naming styles of the Roman higher classes. They preferred names associated with the founders and martyrs of their religion or simple Greek and Latin names. Peter, Paul, John, Timothy, Stephen, and Mary rapidly began to replace the classical names Publius, Tiberius, Titus, Claudius, Julius, etc.

Finally, the fall of the Western Roman Empire in 476 signalled not only the triumph of the barbarians but also witnessed the collapse of many Roman institutions. In the cataclysmic fall of the Roman Empire, the traditional Roman naming patterns were lost forever.

Curiously, Ireland was the first European country, after the fall of Rome, to adopt hereditary family names. Family names have been found in Ireland as early as the beginning of the tenth century; many became fixed during the eleventh and twelfth centuries. Some scholars ascribe this to the fact that Ireland was rapidly converted to Christianity. With the Christian faith came letters and learning, and the advent of scholarship meant that the pedigrees of the great families were recorded in writing at a very early time. The Irish clung to their ancient Hibernian nomenclature till the reign of Queen Elizabeth I, when they were finally pressured by legislation to adopt English surnames.

No instance of a hereditary family name is found in England before the Norman conquest, in 1066. It was not until a century or more after the conquest that hereditary surnames are found in great numbers, and by the end of the fourteenth century family names were generally hereditary.

In Spain, family names were developed in the latter part of the twelfth century and became hereditary by the end of the thirteenth century.

In contrast to the above, family names did not become fixed in Sweden until near the end of the nineteenth century.

In Denmark, the law of May 1828 ordained that children, at baptism, be given not only a first name but also a family name. A second law had to be passed in the late 1860s that made the family name hereditary. And because the Danes were using too many patronymics, the same names appeared over and over again, so that another law had to be passed in 1904 to encourage a greater variety of surnames.

It was not till January 1, 1935, that a Turkish law went into effect making the use of family names compulsory in that country.

Jewish family names began to become common in the tenth and eleventh centuries. There are several important reasons for this development. The rise of cities, to which Jews had moved in growing numbers, was the most important immediate factor. In an urban environment it was impossible for individuals to know one another as they did in villages, and mere personal names no longer sufficed to differentiate them as before. The increase in commerce, too, necessitated a more exact system of naming. This would explain why the main impetus for the spread of surnames came from southern Europe, particularly Venice and the other north and central Italian cities that were centers of medieval commerce. Thus, tradition has it that Jews first adopted surnames in Italy. One family, still extant in the eighteenth century, called itself Adolescenti ("youths") and traced its descent from the captive Jewish youths brought to Rome by Titus after the fall of Jerusalem.

By this time, naming after relatives was quite widespread. Ashkenazim would name after deceased relatives; Sephardim would name after living relatives as well. Italy enjoyed a certain border-state status and was a Sephardic-Ashkenazic cultural mixture. Politically, northern Italy was part of the Holy Roman Empire; in Jewish practice, too, it followed the German Ashkenazi rite. Central and southern Italy was

Sephardic in orientation. Among Jews generally, as a result of the custom of naming children after relatives, many identical personal names appeared in the same family, which made it necessary to add something more to a name to avoid confusion.

All through the Middle Ages surnames were quite common among Spanish and Portuguese Jews, who adopted the practice from the Arabs. And second names soon made their appearance among the Sephardim of France where, as among the other Sephardim, the patronymic type was the most popular. This was formed in various ways: (1) The use of *ibn* ("son of," in Arabic) replaced the Hebrew *ben* among the Arabic-speaking Jews of Spain and North Africa. The most famous examples are Ibn Aknin, Ibn Verga, Ibn Ezra. (2) Another variant was simply to tack one's father's name on to one's own; this was especially common in southern France. Bonet, the son of Abraham, became Bonet Abraham; Shelomo, the son of Vidal, became Shelomo Vidal. (3) In Spain the paternal name, translated into the vernacular, would be used as the family name: Habib ("dear," or "cherished," in Hebrew) became Caro in Spanish; Zemach ("branch," in Hebrew) became the Spanish Crescas; the Hebrew Asher became Maimon ("fortunate," in Arabic), etc., etc.

The Hebrew name Shalom (which means "peace" or "perfect" and is used in greeting) was translated by some Spanish Jews to become Benveniste ("welcome"). Among the Jews of northern Spain and Provence, Shalom was translated to become Barfat, from Berfet, derived from Perfetto ("perfect"). Jews who were exempted from taxes because of services rendered to the king of Spain during the Christian reconquest carried the name Franco ("free"). The Hebrew word Shoshan ("lily") was assumed as a family name by Spanish Jews of Toledo in the form of Ibn Shoshan. The Sassoon family traces its descent to this name.

Italian Jews derived the family name Forti ("strong") from

the Hebrew Yehezkel ("may God strengthen") and Hezekiah ("God is strong"). German Jews coming to Italy were dubbed Tedesco (Italian for "German"). Jews in southern France with the Hebrew names Mazel Tov or Gad ("lucky") assumed the name Astruc, which is Provençal for "born under a lucky star."

Occupations also served as the source of family names. Among Spanish Jews we find Hazan or Chazan ("cantor," in Hebrew), Alfakar ("potter," in Arabic), Zebag ("dyer," in Arabic). Other occupational names derived from Arabic are: Abudraham (literally, "the father of the drachme," a title designating minter or the collector of taxes), Atar ("spice merchant"), Abulafia ("physician"), Tibbon ("straw merchant"). (These last three happen to be among the oldest and most illustrious of Sephardic surnames.) In southern France there were the Hebrew names of Halfan, or Chalfan ("money changer"), Gabbai ("synagogue official"), Kimchi ("flour merchant"); and in Italy, Dayan ("rabbinic judge"), Rofe ("physician"), and the Italian name Cantarini ("cantor").

Many Sephardic family names stem from nicknames based on personal or other characteristics: thus Albo ("white," in Spanish), Bueno ("good," in Spanish), Kassin (from Hebrew *katzin*, "rich"), Petit ("small," in French), etc.

But most surviving Sephardic family names are derived from places of origin. This practice became very widespread after the expulsion of the Jews from Spain and Portugal. At first, the names of localities were preserved, it would seem for reasons of sentiment. Spain has given us Acosta, Alcalay (from Alcola), Belmonte, Cardozo, Cordovero (from Cordova), Espinoza (whence Spinoza), Gerondi, Toledano, Pardo and Prado (from Prado in Castile), Castro, Montalban, Medina, Najara (from Najera), and so on. France is the home of Nantua and Villanova, and Italy of Porto, Trani, Montefiore, Luria (whence the present-day Lurie), Bassan and Bassani (from Bassano in northern Italy), Fano, Modiano and Modena (from

Modena), Norzi (from Norcia), and Finzi (from Faenza). Cape Capsali in southern Greece is the source of the name Capsali.

A most interesting practice among the Jews of medieval Spain, Italy, and southern France—particularly among those who were writers—was to form a surname by translating the name of one's place of origin into Hebrew. Thus Parchi comes from *perah* (Hebrew for "flower") and was adopted by a Jewish writer from Florenza in Spain; Yarchi comes from *yareah* (Hebrew for "moon") and was used by a Jew of Lunel in France; Kaspi was taken from *kesef* (Hebrew for "silver") by a Jew of Argentière; Kochabi, from *kokhab* ("star"), was derived from Estella in Provence; Kansi, from *knesset* ("school"), in Hebrew was the translation of D'Escola among Provençal Jews; and Meati (*mea* in Hebrew means "one hundred") was taken as a family name by Jews from Cento, Italy.

Other surnames designated the quarter of the city in which the bearer lived: hence Portaleone, or "Lion's Gate," a section in the Roman ghetto. A name might indicate both the occupation and place of origin of its bearer: Rofa di Porto (physician [in Hebrew] of Porto, Italy) was the honored leader of his community. His descendants abound today under a corrupted form of that same name: Rappaport.

Among the Ashkenazim in northern Europe the story is quite different. They were more isolated from the Gentiles around them than were the Sephardim in the Mediterranean countries; their political rights were more precarious; and they were not numerous in the larger cities. In Frankfurt on the Main the Jews numbered only seven hundred in the fourteenth century, and there were only about twelve hundred Jews in Prague as late as the sixteenth. Members of communities of this size usually knew one another quite intimately, so there was little need for surnames. In non-Jewish registers, the surname "the Jew" was generally added to the first name, and that was all. In Jewish records we find, besides the common patronymic forms, a prevalence of places of origin: Ephraim of Bonn, Meir of Ruthenberg, Yom Tob of York, Petahiah of Regensberg, Yehiel of Paris, and so on.

In the fourteenth and fifteenth centuries, we come across some family names that already wear their modern forms—that is, the designating preposition is omitted: Moysse Tannenbach and Gabriel Treviess, both of which are based on places of origin. In patronymics we find a Jeckli the son of Jolieb referred to as Jeckli Joliebes.

Though the development of surnames among the Ashkenazi Jews followed patterns similar to those of their Gentile neighbors, there was one basic difference: the Crusades and the subsequent rise of commerce may have provided the impetus for an increase of family names among Christians, but the progress of the Crusaders themselves through France, Germany, and Bohemia brought great suffering and political degradation to the Jewish communities there. And with the deterioration of their political and social status, the spread of family names among the Jews was arrested—as if such names, or the need for them, were a concomitant of material and social advancement. And the increasing isolation of the Jews of western and central Europe, in the late Middle Ages and during the Reformation, from the centers of life around them seems to have continued to keep their need for distinctive names low.

Jewish birth records were not usually kept during the Middle Ages. Even when they were, the fortunes of the community were often such that they were either lost or destroyed. Frequent expulsions and persecutions prevented any written record being retained for any length of time. Generally, knowledge of family descent rarely extended beyond four or five generations. Inscriptions on tombstones provide a more permanent record, and these show us that family names were rather exceptional among Ashkenazi Jews before the late eighteenth century: that is, as long as the Jews were left free to choose them of their own accord. The few choices they did make, however, set a number of precedents that were followed later on, when they were compelled by law to adopt family names.

Throughout the Middle Ages, as we have seen, the Jews relied greatly on patronymics for family names. The name of the scholar Moses Isserles is an example: Isserles is a genitive form of Isserl, which was used as a diminutive of Israel. Another name of the same kind is Moscheles.

Since women were often the breadwinners, many famous Ashkenazim bore as surnames the names of their mothers or other female members of the family: Samuel Eidels, Joel Sirkes (Sirke being a diminutive of Sarah), Moshe Rivkes, Zvi Chayes, etc. Names denoting personal characteristics appear now and then, as the German names Klein ("small"), Lang ("long"), Schwartz ("dark" or "black"), or the Hebrew Jaffe ("beautiful"), and so forth.

Some Jewish last names throw light on historical facts of great interest. For example, the common notion that medieval Jews were exclusively engaged in money lending can be refuted by the fact that such Germanic surnames as Arzt ("doctor"), Becker ("baker"), Metzger ("butcher"), Schreiner ("cabinet maker"), and Schneider ("tailor") survive from before the fifteenth century. Other occupations appear as family names in German and Hebrew, respectively: Apotheker and Rokeach ("druggist" or "dealer in spices"), Schreiber and Sofer ("secretary" or "scribe"), Richter and Dayan ("rabbinic judge"), Lehrer and Melamed ("teacher").

However, most Jewish surnames in the Middle Ages derive from places of origin, with every part of Europe being represented, often in corrupted form. Alsatian Jews coming to Germany were dubbed in German *Welsch* or *der Welsche,* meaning "foreign." When these Jews, driven by persecution, migrated to Poland, Welsch became Wallack, Wallach, or Wloch, which, when their bearers remigrated to Germany, became Block.

Last names formed from abbreviations—a practice never

followed by Gentiles—were derived from the initials of the first name and patronymic as well as from places of origin. Such names were usually conferred on great masters of learning: thus Rashi (*R*abbi *Sh*lomo *I*tzhaki), Rambam (*R*abbi *M*oshe *b*en *M*aimon), Ralbag (*R*abbi *L*evi *b*en *G*erson), and Rashal (*R*abbi *Sh*elomo *L*uria). Among the curious abbreviations derived from places of origin is Ash from *A*lt*sh*ule, the old synagogue of Prague, or from *A*isen*sh*tadt. Other abbreviations commemorate a special event in the life of the family: Bak, from b*ene k*edoshim, "children of martyrs"; Saks, from *zera k*edoshim *S*piro, "descendants of the martyrs of Speyer."

Before leaving the Middle Ages, several observations ought to be made. In our day, the last name is more important than the first: Doe distinguishes John Doe from most of the rest of the world, and John only distinguishes him from other Does. In the Middle Ages, however, the surname served only to help along the personal name in its identifying function: Doe distinguished John Doe from all the other Johns. The primacy of the medieval first name can be discerned in the fact that the monogram of Albrecht Dürer, the famous German painter of the sixteenth century, consisted of a capital "A" and a small "d." Similarly in the works of the *paytanim* (the composers of Hebrew liturgic poetry), who sometimes signed their poems by forming an anagram of their names with the initial letter of each line, it is the first name that is honored in the great majority of cases.

Another sign of the slight regard medieval Jews had for their family names was the ease with which they themselves, or other people, changed them. A name denoting a place of origin might be altered simply because its bearer had moved. Joel Herlingen (Herlingen was the residence of his father) was also called Joel Stein (Stein being his own place of residence).

Jews also used both religious and secular names, first names as well as surnames. A Jew sometimes had one name in the Jewish community and another for civic and business purposes. Simon Heine, the great-grandfather of Heinrich Heine, was also called Simon Bueckeburg, having come from that place. The philosopher Moses Mendelssohn was sometimes called Moses Dessauer, because he came from Dessau.

A classic example of multiple naming is Moses Schuster Kahn, who was also known as Moses Spanier Kahn and Moses Frosch Spanier. Schuster is an occupational surname, denoting, in German, that he was a cobbler by trade; the Hebrew-based name Kahn tells us that he was of priestly lineage; Spanier identified him as having originally come from Spain; Frosh ("frog," in German) indicates that either Moses or his forefather once lived in a house "at the Sign of the Frog."

This disorganized state of affairs as regards Jewish family names created great difficulties for government authorities, and so, when the German states undertook to "emancipate" the Jews at the turn of the eighteenth and nineteenth centuries, they made an effort to regularize Jewish family names by requiring them to adopt fixed and permanent ones.

3

The Compulsory Adoption of Names

UP TO THE END of the eighteenth century the choice of a family name was left to the individual Jew. Many Jews, as we have previously noted, had already adopted family names. This was especially true among the Sephardim of Spain, Portugal, and Italy.

However, the majority of Jews in Germany and eastern Europe still followed the custom of using their personal plus their father's name—Yaakov ben Yitzhak. (A notable exception were the Jews in the landgraviate of Hesse-Cassel who adopted German family names long before they were compelled to do so by law. The names Goldschmid, Heilbrunn, Kugelmann, Katzenstein, Gottschalk, and Schartenberg occur as early as the seventeenth century.)

But a new era was beginning to dawn for Europe, and some of its rays were to touch Jewish life. The eighteenth century has been characterized as the Age of Enlightenment in Europe, but it also witnessed a continuous struggle among the various nations of Europe to maintain a balance of power. National interests had no meaning, and provinces were exchanged and domains rearranged like chess pieces. Both the new ideological climate and the political maneuverings were destined to bring some very important changes in Jewish life, which had remained undisturbed for centuries behind ghetto walls.

Empress Maria Theresa of Austria, who ruled her empire for forty years (1740–1780), was a most fanatic and bigoted monarch. She despised her Jewish subjects to such a degree that she could not stand the sight of them and would grant audiences to Jews from behind a partition. Under her, the Hapsburg monarchy ruled over the largest population of Jews at that time, as a result of the first partition of Poland (1772) which gave Galicia to Austria.

It is an irony of Jewish history that it was Maria Theresa's son and successor, Joseph II, who made the first attempt to sweep medievalism out of Austria. An admirer of Voltaire and a disciple of the Enlightenment, Joseph became an ardent advocate of the new ideology. He permitted Jews to study handicrafts and to engage in agriculture and wholesale commerce. He admitted them into the universities and the army. He abolished the Jewish poll tax, the distinctive garb, and the compulsory wearing of beards. The German language was introduced into Jewish schools, and all communal documents were to be written exclusively in German (at the same time, the use of Hebrew and Yiddish in business transactions and correspondence was prohibited).

In 1787 Emperor Joseph II promulgated an edict ordering the Jews of Galicia and Bucovina to adopt permanent family names, the first such law in Europe.

The third partition of Poland ceded Warsaw and its Jewish population to Prussia. For twelve years (1794–1806) the Prussians occupied Warsaw and during that period imposed German-sounding names on its Polish Jews.

Laws ordering Jews to assume fixed family names were passed in Frankfurt in 1807 and in Baden in 1809. In the French-created Kingdom of Westphalia a decree issued on March 31, 1808, required all Jews to take family names within three months. On July 20 of that year Napoleon decreed a similar requirement for all the Jews in his empire. Both decrees forbade Jews to take names based on localities or to adopt the names of famous families. Still, many Jews got around both these restrictions. When they were prohibited from using the names of well-known geographical sites, they used the names of mountains, rivers, or forests nearby. They even evaded the prohibition against using names of famous families sometimes; thus, some Jews took the name Schoenteil, which is the German translation of Bonaparte.

A Prussian edict of March 11, 1812, emancipated the Jews but made the emancipation conditional upon the adoption of family names within six months. The names chosen were subject to the approval of the authorities. Bavaria followed suit in 1813. This requirement was extended to Posen in 1833, to Saxony in 1834, and to other parts of the Prussian kingdom in 1845.

In the Russian Empire the process of adopting permanent family names was initiated by Czar Alexander's statute in 1804 and was finalized in 1845. Although a decree had required the Jews of Poland to assume family names in 1821, these regulations were not strictly enforced. The 1845 Russian imperial decree finally compelled the Polish Jews to take fixed family names, too.

These new regulations were intended, above all, to serve several practical ends for the governments concerned. The levying of taxes would be expedited by fixed surnames, and so would the conscription of Jewish soldiers. (Historians today see in Emperor Joseph's *Judenordnung* a shrewd maneuver by the monarch to have the Jews serve as the Germanizing element in Poland to offset the Polish influence.) But here was also an opportunity to Westernize, "civilize," and assimilate the Jew. To many an "enlightened" Jew, the adoption of a family name looked to be one more asset in the struggle to secure equal rights and integrate oneself in the Gentile world.

Most Jews, however, resisted the adoption of family

names. The laws regulating the assuming of names were usually part of a larger decree, the purpose of which was to assimilate the Jew. These decrees upset the Jew's life and the course of his traditions, for they regulated not only the economic and civic conditions; they abolished and changed the internal and religious life. Many Jews viewed with apprehension the dissolution of a life-style to which they had grown accustomed over the centuries and in which—oppressive as it may have been—they felt secure. And so they resisted. In many places, the edicts had to be enforced over and over again. Meanwhile, for the government officials in charge, the granting and registering of names proved a new way of extorting money from Jews. Fine-sounding names derived from flowers and gems (Rosenthal, Lilienthal, Edelstein, Diamant, Saphir) came at a high price. Those who could not afford to pay were stuck with such German names as Schmalz ("grease"), Affenkraut ("monkey weed"), Borgenicht ("do not borrow"), Ochsenschwantz ("ox tail"), Temperaturwechsel ("temperature change"), Singmirwas ("sing me something"), Galgenstrick ("gallow's rope"), Verderber ("despoiler"), Eselkopf ("donkey's head"), Taschengreiger ("pocket grasper"), and the like. Just as the use of Hebrew in business transactions was prohibited, so an attempt was made to eliminate all Hebrew elements from names and render their form as "German" as possible. This led to the prohibition of Biblical names, but the prohibition was not strictly enforced, and Jews managed in many cases to evade it.

Where Jews could manage by some device or other to escape the interference of the authorities and choose their own names, they resorted to several methods. When the deadline finally came, many who had delayed opened the Bible at random and chose the first name they could find. We know of one congregation that assembled in the synagogue at the direction of its rabbi, who then opened the prayer book and assigned the first word on the page to the first family, the following word to the second family, and so on down the line. In some cases names were simply invented out of whole cloth; in others they were taken from characters in the popular literature of the day (Sternberg, Morgenthau). In many communities in Hungary, the Jews were divided into four groups, and each group was assigned the name Weiss ("white"), Schwartz ("black"), Gross ("big"), and Klein ("little") respectively. This simplified and expedited the naming process.

But a more popular procedure was to draw on the tribal lineage of the family. Those who were descended from the priestly caste *(kohanim)* became Cohen, Kahn, Barkan ("son of Kahn"), and Katz (the latter an acronym for k*ohen* tz*edek*, "priest of righteousness")—or, in Slavic countries, where there was no "h" sound, Kogen, Kagan, and Kaplan (the last meaning "descended from priests"). The ceremony of the priestly benediction (called in Yiddish "dukhening," from the *dukhen*, the platform on which the *kohanim* stand) is the source of the names Duchan, Duchen, and Duchin. A descendant of Aaron is called in Russian Agranat, in Italian Sacerdóte, and in French Lepretre. A popular belief that both curly headed people and *kohanim* are quick-tempered has made Kraushaar ("curly haired") a name for those of priestly descent.

Those of Levitic descent became Levy, Levin, Levinsky, Levitan, Levitt, Levitansky, and Segal (the latter an abbreviation for *segan leviah*, "member of the Levites"). Variations of Segal are Zoegell, Chagall, and Segalowitch.

Some of the authorities, however, frowned upon these Hebraisms and insisted that Germanic forms be used. Hence we get a bizarre assortment of Hebrew-German combinations: Aronstein, Aronstam, Katzmann, Katzenstein, Cohnheim, Cohnstein, Levinthal, and so forth.

Another method was to make the secular first name or *kinnui* (a sign or symbol of a name as, for example, Lion, or

Leo, for Judah; see Chapter 6), which could easily be adapted to the vernacular, into the family name. Sometimes a corrupted or diminutive form of the Hebrew or Yiddish first name would do for a surname: e.g., Baruch Bendit, Jacob Koppelman. Often the Hebrew first name was simply translated into the vernacular. The idea of "peace" was carried over from Solomon and Shalom into the name Fried and Friedman; the meaning of "great" was transferred from Gedaliah into Grossman; "laughter" is the common element of Itzhak (Isaac) and Lachman; "goodness" is shared by Tuviah and Gutman (Goodman); "strength" is the distinguishing characteristic of Shimshon (Samson) and Starkman; and "light" is the shining feature of Meir and Lichtman.

Such translations were made in every language. For example, Wolf, the *kinnui* of Benjamin, appeared as the Slavic Wilk. In the same way Naphtali, for which the *kinnui* Herz ("hart," in German) was used as a family name, was translated by French Jews into Cerf, while in Slavic countries it became Yellin or Yellinik (Jellinik). (Herz, incidentally, is the root of several names—Herzbach, Herzbrunn, Herzog, Herzfeld, Herzberg. The suffixes were added either for the sheer sake of embellishment or to distinguish one name clearly from another.)

The simplest way of choosing a family name was to create a patronym. Among Austrian and German Jews this was done with the suffix *-sohn,* and among Slavic Jews with the suffix *-vitch:* hence Mendelsohn, Mendelovitch; Abramsohn, Abramovitch; Isaacsohn, Isaakovitch. Jews in Slavic countries also used the suffixes *-ov, -off, -eff,* and *-kin* to denote "descendant of," and to this day we find a host of matronymics and patronymics built on this principle: Baskin (from Basyah, or Batyah), Chaikin (from Chayyah, or Hayyah), Rivkin (from Rivke, or Rebecca), Sorkin (from Sarah), Malkov (from Malkah), Aronoff (from Aaron).

In Germany and the Austro-Hungarian empire, the

mother's name rather than the father's very often served as the
basis of a surname: *Sarassohn, Zirelsohn, Breines, Beiles,
Gitles, Reines, Zeldes, Perles*. And frequently a man would
forsake both his parents to go with his wife: Dienesmann
("husband of Dinah"), Estermann ("husband of Esther"),
Hodesmann ("husband of Hadassah"), Perlmann ("husband of
Perl"). Sometimes, however, it was possible to make a
German-sounding name out of the initials of the Hebrew
patronymic, so that many a *ben* Barukh became Bab, while
ben Chaim (Hayyim) emerged as Bach, and *ben* Rab Nathan as
Brann.

Occupations, of course, became an important source of
derivation among the Ashkenazim when it came to the
formation of new surnames, as these translations from their
Germanic origins show: Becker ("baker"), Fleischer
("butcher"), Breuer ("brewer"), Weber ("weaver"), Farber
("painter"), Goldschmidt ("goldsmith"), Kramer ("merchant"),
Wechsler ("money changer"), Brenner ("distiller"), Gerber
("tanner"). Hundreds of other examples could be cited, and
when we consider that the same principle was followed by
Jews living in many different language areas, we get some idea
of the vast number of occupational names.

This category, incidentally, is even wider than might be
suspected at first, for occupational names were now and then
taken from the material worked with, or from the tools of the
trade. Thus, a tanner might call himself Leder ("leather"), and
a tailor would become Seidenfaden ("silk thread"), Fingerhut
("thimble"), Nadel ("needle"), or Scher ("shears"). A carpenter might choose to be a Nagel ("nail"); a seller of kitchen-
wares or a cook, Ribeisen ("grater"); or a tailor, Biegeleisen
("flat iron").

All occupations, professions, and crafts, from the most
homely to the most exalted, are represented among Jewish
family names. There are, for example, a whole range of
Hebrew-based names deriving from religious occupations:

thus Rabad (an abbreviation of r*esh* a*v* b*eth* d*in,* "head of a rabbinic court") and the same with a suffix, Ravidovitch; Babad (b*en* a*v* b*eth* d*in,* "son of a rabbi"), Rabin, and Rabinovitch; and Motzkin (a descendant of Motz, an abbreviation for m*oreh* tz*edek,* "teacher of righteousness," a title for a rabbi).

The position of sexton is the source of the Germanic names Schulman ("school [synagogue] man"), Klausner ("cloister man"), Shuldine, Diener ("server"), Kleinsinger ("little singer"), Klopman (the man who knocks on the shutters to rouse people for morning worship), and Klapholtz (the rattle used by the sexton to waken the people), and the Slavic for Schulman, Shkolnik (Skolnik), as well as the Hebrew Shames *(shammas),* which means "sexton."

The cantorate provided Kantor, Singer, Chazan ("cantor," in Hebrew), Grossinger ("main singer," in German), Schulsinger ("synagogue singer," in German), Spivak (Slavic for "cantor"), Voorsanger (Dutch for "cantor"), Cantarini ("cantor," in Italian), Schatz (abbreviation for *shaliah tzibbur,* "representative of the congregation"), and Schen (abbreviation of *shaliah neeman,* "faithful representative").

From the profession of ritual slaughterer came the Yiddish Schechter, the Hebrew Shochet, Bodek ("inspector," [of animals] in Hebrew), Resnick (Slavic for slaughterer), Shub (abbreviation for s*hohet* u*bodek*—"slaughterer and inspector"), and Menaker (from the Hebrew "porger of meat," one who removes the hindquarter sinews and veins, which are prohibited).

Teachers became Melamed and Lehrer (in Hebrew and German, respectively) and the Slavic Uchitel. The one who preached is the Magid and the reader of the Torah scroll is the Lehner. The religious supervisor *(mashgiah)* is the source of the names Neeman and Naimon ("trustworthy," in Hebrew) and its German equivalent Wahrman and the Russian Wernik.

The barber-surgeon, who was often the only medical

practitioner in the community, is represented by the names, Bader, ("barber," in German), Feldscher ("surgeon," in German; it becomes Felsher through Yiddish), Cirulnik ("barber," in Russian), and Lanzner (from *Lanze*, "lancet," used for blood-letting). The name Gelfman, which is the Russian form for Helfman ("assistant," in German) also meant a barber-surgeon in Yiddish; Spitalny, too, the Polish for a hospital director, was used in Yiddish as the title of the person in charge of the *hekdesh*, the community infirmary and poor house, and came to mean barber-surgeon, as well.

Personality and physical characteristics, as we have seen, had always been a source of informal Jewish surnames (and of non-Jewish as well: Richard the Lion-Hearted, Charles the Wise, Frederick Barbarossa—i.e., of the red beard). It was to be expected, therefore, that many Jews would adopt surnames of this type when the new laws came into effect. Germanic names like Kurtz ("short"), Stark ("strong"), Schnell ("fast"), Gross ("big") are common examples. We also find a large group of names determined by the color of one's hair: the Germanic Schwartz (Slavic: Chorney) for black, Weiss (Slavic: Bialik) for white, Roth ("red"), Braun ("brown"), Gelber or Geller ("yellow"), Graubart ("gray beard").

Some Jews simply registered the nicknames by which they were known in the Jewish community with the local authorities. Sometimes, however, it took a full purse to persuade the civil magistrate to agree; complimentary names like the German Kluger ("wise") or Frohlich and Lustig ("happy") came at a high price. One group of family names was supplied by the German names of the days of the week, as well as of seasons—Frühling ("spring"), Sommer ("summer"), Sonntag ("Sunday"), Dienstag ("Tuesday")—referring presumably to the time of birth or, perhaps, to the occasion on which the name was officially registered.

However, most Ashkenazi family names, like those of the Sephardim, point to place or origin, and so we find innumerable provinces, cities, villages, and hamlets all over Germany, Austria, Poland, western Russia, Hungary, and other countries represented among extant Jewish surnames.

Some of the most popular place names are: Auerbach, Bachrach, Bamberger, Brody, Dreyfuss (Alsation corruption of Trèves, the French name for Trier in the Rhineland), Dresner (Dresden), Epstein, Florsheim, Ginzberg, Wiener, Weil, Landau, Spiro (Spayer from Speyer, whence also Shapiro), Lemberger, Lasker, Kalischer, Ellbogen, Horowitz (Slavic: Gurovitz), Gumbiner. Other names indicate an area or country of origin, e.g., the Germanic Schwab (from Swabia), Schlesinger (from Silesia), Frank (from Franconia), Posner (from Posen), Pollack (from Poland), Litauer (from Lithuania), and so on.

Several interesting historical details are involved in Jewish place names. Nürnberg, for example, is seldom found as a Jewish name. Having been expelled from Nürnberg in 1499, Jews were permitted to spend only one day at a time in that city, if they had business there; at dusk they had to leave. Fürth, some three and one-half miles away, was the most convenient place to reside for Jews doing business in Nürnberg, but it wasn't the only one. The Free City, so proud to be *Judenrein* (free of Jews), tolerated Jews in a number of villages within its own territory. This neat solution to Nürnberg's Jewish problem in past centuries lives on in surnames like Schnaittacher, Ottensosser, Fürth, and Fürther.

It isn't always easy to determine whether a particular name stems from a town or not. Thus, Steinberg, Goldberg, Greenberg, and Rosenberg happen to be names of real places, but Levinstein and Aronthal are inventions. Nor need the possession of a place name mean that the bearer actually was a resident of the place designated. Many Jews called Moses selected the place name Mosbach because of its phonetic rather than geographic connection. The family name Berlin has, in most cases, nothing to do with the German city. It is a patronymic of Ber or Berl. Berlin simply means "the son of Berl."

In the same way members of the family Paris never laid eyes on Gay Paree! Jews called Paris originated in the town of Parysow, in Poland. Nor do most Hollanders come from Holland. They come from a number of villages named Hollendry, in Lithuania and Poland, that were established by Dutch dairy farmers in the sixteenth century.

And finally, the family name London is really the Hebrew word *lamden* ("scholar"), by which the bearer was known in the Jewish community. But the naming authorities confused London with Lamden. Some officials compounded the error by giving a *lamden* the name Englander on the assumption that London and England belong together.

4

"On the Doorposts of Your House and on Your Gates"

ONE OF THE MOST important developments in the history of Jewish family names took place in Frankfurt on the Main, where the Jews were compelled to live in a ghetto called the Judengasse and families were registered according to the houses they occupied, the right to live there being closely tied up with the ownership of one's house.

In medieval German cities, as elsewhere in Europe, houses were not numbered; few people then could read letters or numbers anyhow. It was the custom in most places to identify a house by a sign hung outside. These colorful and picturesque house signs seem to have had a particular attraction for Jews; no matter how far the Jew had traveled from his original house in Frankfurt, he still valued its memory. So strong, in fact, was the love of the Jews for their house signs that they became part of family tradition and, like their forefathers in the days of the Roman Caesars who put signs in the catacombs, the Jews of Frankfurt and Prague carved house signs on their gravestones.

The rationalizing French introduced the practice of numbering houses, and by the end of the eighteenth century house signs had all but disappeared in Germany. When, in 1776, the houses in Frankfurt's Judengasse were ordered to be numbered, there was such bitter resistance that the city council fined the whole Jewish community. This is all the more significant because there is no evidence of any Gentile community shedding tears at the passing of its house signs. (Perhaps no other people in pre-nineteenth-century Europe were so conservative fundamentally as the Jews, who tended to make habitual usage sacred usage.) It is therefore small wonder that so many house signs found their way into Jewish family names from the sixteenth century on.

At first, house signs were illustrations of the owner's first name. Thus the house of a Jew known as Wolf would be called *zum Wolf* ("at Wolf's"), and its sign would bear a picture of a wolf and the house itself designated "At the sign of the Wolf." To this day European hotels, inns, and pubs use such signs, and they were also common in Colonial America. Many German Jewish first names which had been taken from animals lent themselves very well to pictorial representation, and so we find homes with such designations as: *Gans* ("goose"); *Baer* ("bear"); *Loeb* ("lion"). All these animal names, it must be remembered, were first names.

Sometimes a slight modification had to be made in order to represent the home-owner's name by a picture. The diminutive of Isaac was commonly Seckl. If an owner was named Isaac, he would have a sickle painted on his house sign, feeling that *Sickel* ("sickle," in German) could easily stand for Seckl. In the same way the figure of a blackbird *(Amsel)* adorned the houses of Jews called Amschel (which is a corrupted form of Anselm).

But not all personal names could be represented by pictures. In such cases Jews often borrowed from the house signs of Gentile neighbors. These borrowings were eventually incorporated into family names and are still extant.

Almost two hundred house signs have come down to us from the Frankfurt Ghetto and the following are some of the family names that they represent: Apfelbaum ("apple tree"), Birnbaum ("pear tree"), Blum ("flower"), Buxbaum ("box tree"), Druck or Drach ("dragon"), Eichel, Eichler ("acorn"), Einhorn ("unicorn"), Engel, Engler ("angel"), Flasch, Flesch, Flaschin ("flask"), Frosch ("frog"), Greenhut ("green hat"), Gruenbaum ("green tree"), Hirschhorn ("deer antlers"), Kestenbaum ("chestnut tree"), Kolben and Kulp ("club"), Nussbaum ("nut tree"), Ochs ("ox"), Rebhun, Rephun, Rebhuhn, Raphan ("partridge"), Riese, Reese, Reiss, Reis, Ries ("giant"), Rothschild ("red shield"), Scheuer ("barn"), Schwartzschild ("black shield"), Spiegel ("mirror"), Stern ("star"), Storch ("stork"), Strauss (either "ostrich" or "flower bouquet"), and Taube ("dove").

Some of these house-sign names may also have other derivations; for example, the name Ochs could derive as well from the legend of Saul who became a Jewish king of Poland, as was indicated previously in Chapter 1. It could have still another derivation as the *kinnui* for Joseph, since it means "bull" in German and Joseph is described as a young bull in Deuteronomy.

There is a particularly interesting history behind the name Adler ("eagle," in German). The legendary phoenix, which was said to be reborn out of its own ashes, was identified with the eagle on the basis of Psalm 103:5 ("renewing your youth like an eagle's"). It became the symbol of Jewish survival, and this made it popular as a house sign and then as a surname. Some Adlers, however, who are *kohanim* selected this name because the outstretched hands of a *kohen* in reciting the priestly blessing resembles the wings of the eagle.

One family in Frankfurt that was of priestly descent and known as Cahn took for its house sign the picture of a boat (*Kahn* is "boat" in German). Later, other members of the same family used the sign of a ship—*Schiff*, in German—so that what was originally the Hebrew Kahn became the German Schiff. Some Schiffs took their name from an earlier form of *Schiff*, which in Middle High German meant "vial," and vials were on the house signs of apothecaries or physicians.

A levitic family selected the house sign for *Kann* ("jug"), because the Levites pour water over the hands of the *kohanim* in preparation for the recitation of the priestly blessings.

The most famous house-sign name which Frankfurt has given us is, of course, the name Rothschild. House Number 148 in the Judengasse bore a red shield. Research has brought to our attention some interesting facts about the Rothschild name. The ancestor of the Rothschilds originally lived in a house marked *zum rothen Hahn* ("at the sign of the red cock") and only later moved to the house of the red shield. Further investigation revealed that the former name of the house of the red shield was really *zum grünen Schild* ("at the green shield"). It would appear that a second coat of paint made all the difference.

Those who bear the Germanic family names Elefant, Helfand, Helfant, Elfand (Slavic: Gelfand, Gelfant) will be interested to discover that house signs have been found showing that what our forefathers called an "elephant" was the picture of a camel.

House signs are also responsible for the prevalence of fish names in Jewish family names: e.g., Fisch ("fish"), Lachs ("salmon"), Hecht ("pike"), Karp or Carpeles. But the fish can be traced to other seas as well. Jewish inhabitants of the city of Ryback (meaning "place of fishes") called themselves by the names of various fish. Many whose first name was Ephraim used the *kinnui* Fischel as a family name because in the Bible Jacob told Ephraim that his seed would multiply as the fish in the sea (Genesis 48:16). But some Ephraims fancifully substituted the names of different species of fish. Hence, we get such Germanic fish names as Blaugrundel ("blue goby"), Forell ("trout"), Walfisch ("whale"), Zander ("perch" or "pike"), the Polish Karash ("carp"), and the Slavic Karassick ("little fish").

There were Jonahs who adopted names of fish because of the story of the whale, and there were Joshuas who did likewise because the Biblical Joshua was the son of Nun (*nun* being the Hebrew for "fish").

5

Names Created out
of the Alphabet

A UNIQUE INNOVATION in the history of family names was introduced by the Jews. This was the use of acronyms or abbreviations to form a name. We have already seen how famous scholars and teachers in the early Middle Ages became renowned and were known by their acronyms—Rashi (*R*abbi *Sh*lomo *I*tzhaki), Rambam (*R*abbi *M*oshe *b*en *M*aimon), Ran (*R*abbi *N*issim). This process continued through the centuries with such names as Schach (*Sh*abbetai *C*ohen), Bach (*J*oel Sirkes was known by the title of his book *B*eth *Ch*adash), Malbim (*M*eir *L*ayb *b*en Yechiel *M*ichel), Marshak (*M*orenu *R*av *Sh*lomo *K*luger), etc.

When the time came for Jews to assume permanent family names, many created names out of interesting combinations of letters. Some were patronymics, and we have hundreds of such combinations. One advantage of such creations was that it afforded the opportunity for Jews to preserve the Hebrew element of the name without disclosing the Hebrew word. Many government officials frowned upon or actually forbade the use of any Hebrew in the naming process. Thus, a name like Nachmanson or Nachmans would not be acceptable. But an ingenious creation of a Hebrew acronym, such as Bran or Brann (*b*en *R*eb *N*achman, "the son of Reb Nachman," i.e.,

Nachmanson), preserved the intrinsic element of the Hebrew patronymic while causing no problems with the government naming commission. To the Austrian naming official, Brann looked and sounded German.

Some of the most common patronymic acronyms are Baram (*ben Reb Meir*), Baratz (*ben Reb Tzabok*), Bard, Barth, Bradt, Bardowicz (*ben Reb David*), Barg (*ben Reb Gershon*), Barlas (*ben Reb Layb Sofer*, "son of Layb the scribe"), Barmak (*ben Reb Moshe Kalman*), Barmash (*ben Reb Moshe Shmuel*), Barch and Brach (*ben Reb Chayim*), Barmat (*ben Reb Mattis*, Barshay (*ben Reb Shmuel Yosef*), Barza (*ben Reb Zalman Aaron*), Braf (*ben Reb Feivel*), Bram (*ben Reb Moshe*), Brat (*ben Reb Tuviah*), Brill (*ben Reb Yehuda Layb*), Brim (*ben Reb Yitzhak Meir*), Bruck, Brock, Brockmann (*ben Reb Kalman*), Bry (*ben Reb Yisrael*), Basch (*ben Shimshon*), Brasch, Brosch, Brisch (*ben Reb Shimshon*), and Bad, Badt (*ben David*).

Sometimes a man was the son-in-law of a distingushed member of the community and was thus known. We have a number of acronyms derived from such a relationship: Charap (*Chatan* [*hatan*] *Reb Pinkhas*, "son-in-law of Pinkhas"), Charmatz (*Chatan Reb Moshe Tzvi*), and Charney (*Chatan Reb Nahum Yosef*).

Priestly descent (in addition to the already mentioned Katz, which stands for *kohen tzedek*, "priest of righteousness") was indicated by Casdan, Kashdan (*kohanim shluhe de-rahmana ninhu*, "priests are the messengers of the Merciful God") and Maza (*mizera Aaron*, "from the seed of Aaron").

Titles of rabbinic and communal leadership are also found in family names represented by acronyms: Dym (*dayan umelitz*, "judge and defender"), Metz (*moreh tzedek*, "teacher of righteousness"—a title for a rabbi), Romm (*rosh metivta*, "head of the *yeshivah*"), Gam (*goveh medinah*, "tax collector of the province" or "treasurer of the community"), and Getz (*gabbai tzedekah*, "official in charge of charity funds").

Bak, or Beck, stands for the acronym *bene kedoshim*,

"descendants of martyrs"; Zaks, or Saks, for *zera kodesh shemo*, "his name descends from martyrs," or *zera kodesh Stendal*, "descendants of the martyr of Stendal," or *zera kodesh Speyer*, "descendants of the martyr of Speyer."

A scholar would be addressed in writing by the words *maalat kevod torato*, "esteemed and honored man of Torah," and from this salutation we get the name Macht. In the same way, a person's name in a letter would be followed by the words *sheyihye leorekh yamim tovim*, "may he live long and good days," and this gave us the name Schalit. An Atlas selected the opening verse of Psalm 73 *Akh tov lyisrael selah*, "may God be good to Israel"; and a Shick declared *shem yisrael kodesh*, "the name of Israel is holy"; while a few with the name Wallach affirmed *veahavta leraekha kamokha*, "love your neighbor as thyself."

The names of cities were often abbreviated in a unique way in Hebrew and Yiddish correspondence or by the printers of Hebrew books. These standardized abbreviations later became permanent family names when Jews adopted them to indicate their place of origin. *Frosch, Pasch, Presch* (the "f" and "p" become interchanged in unvocalized Hebrew or Yiddish) indicate one who came from either *Fraustadt*, in Posen, or *Freistadt*, in Silesia. Lash is an abbreviation for *Lichtenstadt*, in Bohemia. Nash represents *Nicolsburg* or *Neustadt*. Basch is an acronym for *Bochstein, Burgkunstadt*, or *Borkenstein*. Ash, or Asch, indicates the communities of *Aisenstadt* (in Burgenland), the *Altschul* (in Prague), or *Amsterdam* (pronounced in Yiddish and Hebrew *Amshterdam*.)

Finally, Pach and Pech stand for *pituhe hotem*, "the engraver of seals"; Stamm is the abbreviation of *sofer tefillin mezuzot*, "scribe of phylacteries and mezuzahs"; and Michtam is an acronym for *Meir kotev tefillin mezuzot*, "Meir, the scribe of phylactery and mezuzah parchments."

When it was originally assumed, the name created out of

the letters of the alphabet had a great deal of meaning to the one who fashioned it. Over the years, however, much of the meaning of such names has been lost and their special relevance is no longer known even to the members of the family, except for the very few in which a careful record has been kept to preserve its origin.

6

Gentille to Yente, Menahem to Mendel

FIRST NAMES MAKE A fascinating subject. They are a very important part of Jewish family names, since, as we have seen, a substantial number of family names was derived from patronymics, matronymics, the names of wives, the names of fathers-in-law, and the formation of acronyms involving first names. No study of Jewish names would, therefore, be complete without a review of the origins, the development, and the metamorphoses of first names.

There is another interesting aspect to the study of first names, especially meaningful to a student of folklore. All superstitions surrounding names among Jews involve only first names, and Judaism has developed some remarkable apotropaisms (an attempt to ward off illness, death, or other calamity) that have created many of the first names and name forms we use today (and that have also become part of our family names).

For Jews, first names are inevitably something more than convenient labels for identification, mere tags to facilitate intercourse in a civilized society. Among us they take on a highly charged symbolic value, as the feverish name coinings and Hebraizations of old names in the State of Israel in the past few years tell us, or our own searchings for a "suitable" name for a newborn infant. So it is that Jewish names can serve as clues for deciphering the cultural patterns of Jewish history: from them we can determine whether people's sentiments inclined toward religious separateness or assimilation or Jewish nationalism. We can tell when the Jews are loyal to the Hebrew language and when indifferent. And names also reveal something about the political and economic situations of Jews through the centuries.

It is a strong tradition among most American Jews to name their children after departed relatives. And yet we find no trace of this custom in the Bible. In ancient days the name a Jew gave his child was generally connected with some event, familial or public, that had happened at or near his birth. The name usually took on a symbolic meaning, denoting a wish for the newborn infant's good fortune, expressing thanks to God, and so forth.

Many of the ancient names are theophoric, containing the name of God, and recording that God gives (Elnathan, Jonathan, Nathaniel), increases the family (Yosef, Eliasaph), is gracious (Jochanan, Elhanan, Hananel), has mercy (Yerahmiel), blesses (Berakhiah), loves (Yedidyah), helps (Elazar, Azariah), benefits (Gamliel), is strong (Uzziel, Uzziah), comforts (Nehemiah), heals (Raphael), hears (Elishama, Samuel), remembers (Zechariah), lives (Yehiel), judges (Elishaphat, Jehoshaphat, Shephatiah, Shaphat), is king (Elimelech, Malkiel), is great (Gedaliah), is incomparable (Michael).

A first-born child would be given the name Bekhorath, if a girl, and Bekher, for a boy (first-born), or Jephthah (God opens [the womb]); or a child would be named for animals or plants: Rachel (ewe), Caleb (dog), Shaphan (cony), Jonah (dove), Zipporah (bird), Deborah (bee), Hadassah (myrtle), Habakkuk (a garden plant).

Usually, it would appear, the mother chose the name (as in the case of Jacob's sons and the prophet Samuel); sometimes the father selected it (as in the case of Abraham's sons). Often, as in the naming of Moses and King Solomon, persons other than the parents were the name givers. In remote antiquity, the custom was to name a male infant immediately upon birth (a practice still followed by the Arabs); later on, a boy received his name at the ceremony of circumcision (see Luke 1:59, 2:21).

In the early Biblical period first names were proper names in the full sense of the term, being the exclusive possession of the person upon whom they were first conferred. Every child bore a name uniquely his and coined on the occasion of his birth; no one would ever use that name again. Over a period of a thousand years we find no recurrence of the names of Abraham, Isaac, Jacob, Moses, David, Solomon, etc. Even in the royal family no names were repeated. Not one of the twenty-one kings of Judah was named after David, first of the dynasty. In the lists of the high priests of the First Temple (Ezra 7 and 1 Chronicles 6) no name is repeated.

With but one possible exception we do not find in the Bible any instance of, or reference to, the custom of naming children after parents or grandparents, deceased or alive, at any time before the Babylonian exile. This absolute and persistent silence about such a custom strongly suggests that not only did such a custom not exist, but that there were objections to the practice; it was therefore intentionally avoided.

In the later Biblical period names begin to be repeated, and later still we find the Talmud (Yoma 38b) prohibiting the use of the name of a wicked person. This prohibition is based on the commentary of Rabbi Elazar on Proverbs 10:7, "The memory of the righteous shall be for a blessing, but the *name of the wicked shall rot.*" But Jews, it would seem, never abided by this prohibition. Even rabbis in the Talmudic period disregarded it. Thus, we find several high priests and tannaim who bore the name Ishmael. (In the Bible, Ishmael is classed among the wicked, and in rabbinic literature he is a symbol of impiety, though some rabbis considered him to have turned penitent at the end of his life.) Menahem, which was the name

of a king of Israel (2 Kings 15:17 et seq.), is found only once in
the Bible; about him the Bible says: "And he did that which
was evil in the sight of the Lord; he departed not all his days
from the sins of Jeroboam." Yet many tannaim and amoraim
were named Menachem, and it is a very common name even
today. On the other hand, the names of such pious figures as
the prophets Habakkuk, Zephaniah, and Malachi completely
disappeared among Jews after the Biblical era. If there are
special reasons why some names have withstood the test of
time, and not others, scholars have not been able to discover
them.

In the early Biblical period, Jewish names are Hebrew
names. But in the period following the destruction of the First
Temple and the carrying off of the Jews into the Babylonian
captivity, foreign names and modifications begin to make their
appearance. From this period date many of the traditional
modes of Jewish name-giving, as well as that process of
admixture and combination which has resulted in the bizarre
assortment of names borne by Jews today.

During the sojourn by the waters of Babylon, and even in
the first generation after the return, the Jews displayed two
contrary tendencies, one nationalist and the other assimila-
tionist. One section of the exiles was full of a fierce patriotic
fervor, as evidenced by the loyal devotion to the Hebrew
language and the pure Biblical names they bestowed on their
children. Throughout the later books of the Bible, in Ezra,
Nehemiah, and Chronicles, the old Hebrew names of the
patriarchal era—Joseph, Benjamin, Simeon—reappear. These
early Pentateuchal names nostalgically recall olden heroic
times.

This devotion to Judaism was not only a looking back to
the glorious past; for in addition to reviving disused names,
which had been half forgotten or never popular, the Jewish
patriots of the period created Hebrew names that do not
appear in the earlier books of the Bible. These names—

Nehemiah, Chasadiah, Pedaiah, Melatiah, etc.—express the sentiments of the people in an era of transition, sentiments of hope, consolation, thanksgiving, joy, and trust in the Almighty. But few of these new names are current today.

At the same time, side by side with this patriotic emphasis on Hebrew tradition, there was an opposite tendency to imitate and assimilate foreign forms. The tendency reveals itself in the Aramaic forms that many names acquire during this period (when the Aramaic language had begun to spread over Western Asia and Palestine). We find names in Ezra, Nehemiah, and Chronicles with the Aramaic ending *ai*. Even names that have a Hebrew root are converted into an Aramaic form, as for example: Piltai (from Pelatiah), Shammai (from Shemaiah), Atlai (from Ataliah), Adlai (from Adaliah). We also come across names entirely and directly Aramaic, as well as names borrowed by the Jews from neighboring peoples. Persian-Babylonian names, brought back from the Exile, make their first appearance at this time. Two names in this last category, Mordecai and Shabbetai, have remained popular to this day despite their pagan origin. (Mordecai means "a devotee of the god Marduk" and Shabbetai means "one named in honor of the planet Saturn.")

During the period of Alexander the Great's rule, new Hebrew names continued to be invented. Examples of these occur in the early Mishnah: Shatach, Admon, Perachiah. But most of the Jewish names of the time were Aramaic, with the members of the aristocracy beginning to use Greek names. Even the first scholar of the Mishnah bore the Greek name of Antigonos.

In the Hasmonean period, when Hellenistic culture dominated the Mediterranean world, we find a widespread use of Greek names among the Jews. Jews even bore the name of their fiercest persecutor, Antiochus the Seleucid, the Greek-Syrian emperor against whom the Maccabees had successfully rebelled. Greek names were employed by Jews for many

centuries after the destruction of the Second Temple by the
Roman Titus in 70 c.e.; in the Mishnah and Talmudic
literature we find many tannaim and amoraim with such
Greek names as Alexander, Theodorus, Dosa, Nanos, Nak-
dimon, Polemo, Pappos, Patros, Symmachos, Tarfon, Todos,
etc., and other Jews who bear the names Demetrios, Nicanor,
Philo, Philippos, Ptolmeos, Stephanos, Theophilos, The-
odosios, Kalonymos, Zeno, etc.

Following the Roman conquest of Palestine, a strong Latin
influence made itself felt, though it was never so extensive as
the Greek. In the Mishnaic and Talmudic literatures (especially the Palestinian Talmud), we encounter many rabbis
with Latin names: Drusus, Marinus, Valens, Romanus, Justus,
and, *mirabile dictu,* in several places in the Palestinian
Talmud mention is made of a Rabbi Titus! There were Jews
who even bore the names of the pagan Roman gods, Apollo,
Bacchus, and Castor, and other Latin names such as Agrippa,
Marcus, Julius, Justinus, Rufus, Tiberinus, Tiberius, Crispus,
Dulcius, Julianus, However, the Persian-Aramaic names of
previous times continued to predominate in the Talmudic
period. We even find Zriko and Ashtur, names of Babylonian
gods, used as Jewish first names. We also find the names of the
Jewish calendar months Tammuz and Tebeth used as first
names.

The custom of using a non-Jewish name as a companion
and addition to one's Hebrew name originated several centuries before the destruction of the Second Temple. In the
later books of the Bible we encounter such double names as
Hadassah Esther and Daniel Belshazzar; Hananiah, Mishael,
and Azariah are also called Shadrach, Meshach, and Abed-
nego. During the period of Greek influence it became
customary to have two Hebrew names (a practice still
followed today); we find such combinations as Mahalalel
Judah, Sarah Miriam, and Johanan Joseph. Sometimes a
Hebrew and an Aramaic name were used together. During

this period, too, the linking of a Jewish with a non-Jewish name became more and more the fashion. When Jews adopted Greek as their vernacular in the third century B.C.E., Greek names became increasingly popular. Beginning among the Hellenizing Jewish assimilationists, the use of Greek names gradually spread to the traditionalists. All the Hasmonean kings had a dual Hebrew-Greek name: Johanan-Hyrcanos; Yannai-Alexander; Judah-Aristobolos; Shlomit-Alexandra.

At first, the non-Jewish names were used only in relations with non-Jews. One's Greek name was a direct translation of one's Hebrew name, with Tuvia ("God is good") becoming Ariston or Agathon; Ezra ("help") being metamorphosed into Boethus; Zadok ("just") into Justus; Yedidyah ("beloved of God") into Philo; Nathaniel ("God has given") into Theodorus. Eliakim and Joshua became Alcimus and Jason respectively, because of the similarity in sound. Menahem masqueraded as Menelaus. Gradually, however, the non-Jewish name became the more important one, and finally the only name. When we come upon scholars mentioned in the Mishnah and Talmud with purely Greek names, we must assume they had no other. The rabbis of the Talmud deplored this situation, but to no avail.

Some names of the Talmudic era were authentic Hebrew names and readily recognizable as such, but Hellenized in form or spelling. Joseph appears in the form of Jose; Levi as Levites; Yitzhak as Isak; Shimon as Simon; etc.

A small percentage of feminine proper names were Hebrew; many were Aramaic, e.g., Uma, Martha, Yalta (an Aramaic form of the Hebrew Ayalah). Some feminine Latin and Greek names were used: Alexandra, Berenice, Doris, Beruria (Aramaized form of Veluria). Women were for the most part excluded from political and business life, so that there was less need for Hellenizing or Romanizing their names.

In the Talmudic period, the strong influence of Greek and Roman culture acted to reduce the number of Hebrew names, though there was never any danger, of course, of their being extinguished. We find obscure Biblical names suddenly grown popular because of the distinction won by certain of their bearers, as in the case of Hillel and Gamliel. New Hebrew names not found in the Bible, such as Akabiah, Akashiah, Akiba, Meir, Nahman, Ahavah, Sason, and Nehunyah, came to the fore at this time. Throughout the Talmudic period most Jews did not hesitate to give their children non-Jewish names, and it is reported of the Jews outside of Palestine that the vast majority of them had names like the Gentiles (Gittin 11b).

In post-exilic times and, especially beginning with the Hellenistic period, a remarkable change takes place in the practice of selecting names for Jewish children: people begin to name a child after a deceased relative.

The custom of naming children after ancestors was prevalent among the Egyptians. This practice was picked up by Palestinian Jews who came in contact with Egypt in the post-exilic era. Jews who served in the military colony on the island of Elephantine in the Nile in the fifth century B.C.E. also appear to have borrowed this custom from their Egyptian neighbors. It is reasonable to assume that from the Elephantine Jews the practice spread to Palestine, if indeed the Jews in Palestine did not get it from the Egyptians directly. (The alternation of the names of Onias and Simon in the high priestly family from 332 to 165 B.C.E. indicates the practice in some form.) At first, naming a child after a dead relative was confined to the royal family and aristocracy. Among the Hasmoneans we find a recurrence of the names of Judah, Johanan, and Jonathan; among the Patriarchs of Judea we find two Hillels, three Judahs, six Gamliels, and four Simeons. Other scholars begin to imitate the practice popularized by the Hillelites and we find Halafta son of Rabbi Jose ben Halafta, and Hyrcanos son of Eliezer ben Hyrcanos. Gradually the custom spread to the common people, and it has been followed to this day. The practice was well established by the first century C.E., as we can see from Luke 1:59–61, where a departure from it occasions surprise.

In the Talmudic period, not only did people name their children after departed ancestors, they also named children after living parents or grandparents, relatives or friends. The Talmud (Shabbat 134a and Hullin 47b) records that Rabbi Nathan the Babylonian saved the life of two boys because of his expertise in the procedure of circumcision, and they were named after him. Rabbi Elazar ben Shimon also had boys named after him (Baba Metzia 84b).

Early in the Middle Ages the Jews began to give their children Biblical names that had not been used for eight hundred years: Abraham, Moses, Aaron, David, Solomon, Isaiah, Amnon, Elhanan, Barukh, Noah.

At this time, too, the practice of giving special names to children born on certain days or during certain holidays became widespread among Jews. This custom was already prevalent in the Christian community: boys born on Sunday were called Dominick; during Easter, Pasquale; girls born on Christmas were called Natalie. In like manner, boys born on Saturday were called Sabbetai by Jewish parents; children born in the Purim season were called Mordecai, Esther, or Malkah ("queen," in Hebrew); boys born on Purim or Hanukkah were called Nissim ("miracles"—the Hebrew prayer recited on these holidays is called *al hanissim*, "We thank you for miracles"); Yom Tov (which became Bondi and Bondia in France and Italy, and which means "holy day," in Hebrew) was conferred on children born during a festival; boys born during Passover were called by the name of the festival, Pesah; those born during Nisan, the month in which Passover occurs, were called Nisan; a boy born or circumcised on Yom Kippur was called Rahamim ("mercy," "compassion"); one born on the Ninth of Av or the week following that annual day of mourning would be given the name Menahem or Nahman (both mean "comforter" or "consolation"); among the Sephardim, children born on the Feast of Lights were called Hanukkah, and this is a common name even today among Grusinian, Persian, and Bokharan Jews.

Until the twelfth century, following the custom of Talmudic days, the Jews of Babylonia continued to use Aramaic and Persian names. A roster of the names of the Geonim, the heads of the academies of Sura and Pumbedita, shows that new Aramaic and Persian names were continually being invented. Since Babylonia was then under Islamic rule and influence, Arabic names also occur. Thus one of the Exilarchs is named Josiah Hassan.

In the Middle Ages, giving the name Messiah to a child expressed the hope of each mother that she was giving birth to the Messiah. Thus we find Moshiah ("Messiah") as a personal name among Bokharan, Persian, and Greek Jews. A hint to the Messiah is also evident in the name Menahem Tzion ("comforter of Zion"), which became popular among the Jews of Germany in the Middle Ages.

All the epithets of "the child born to us" (Isaiah 9:5) were attributed to the Messiah and were used for naming children—*pele yoetz* ("wonderful in counsel"), *el gibbor* ("God is mighty"), *avi ad* ("everlasting Father"), and *sar shalom* ("prince of peace"). Yoetz is a name found among Ashkenazim. We already find Sar Shalom as a name of a Gaon of Sura in the middle of the ninth century.

Zemach ("branch," "shoot") is also a Messianic name (see Isaiah 4:2 and especially Zechariah 3:8 and 6:12). In French the name appears in the form Croissant and in Spain the name is Crescas. Zemach is found regularly as a Jewish name to this day.

Mevaser ("bearer of good tidings") (see especially Isaiah 52:7: "How beautiful upon the mountains are the feet of him who brings good tidings, who announces peace, who brings tidings of good, who announces salvation [*yeshua*], who says to Zion: 'Your God reigns!' "), and Yeshua, or Joshua ("salvation") from the same verse was also used as a Messianic name.

Shiloh, too, has a Messianic nuance and was used as a first name. The name appears in Genesis 49:10 in a verse dealing with the royal house of the tribe of Judah and has been esoterically understood by Rashi and others as referring to the Messiah.

Finally, the name David, as we have seen above, is used only once in the entire Bible. It does not appear at all in the Talmudic era. It first begins to reappear in the Gaonic period, and from then on it has remained one of the most popular first names among Jews. Its reintroduction may also be associated with the Messianic hope and yearning of the Jewish people.

From the twelfth century onward, so widespread was the use of non-Jewish names that the rabbis decreed that every Jewish boy must be given a purely Jewish name at his circumcision. Thus the use of two names became the custom: a sacred name *(shem hakodesh)* by which a Jew was called up to read the Torah and which was employed in documents of a religious nature *(ketubot* and *gittin)*; and a non-Jewish name, called the *kinnui,* for civil and business purposes. This rabbinic statute is valid to this day.

In the category of religious names were included not only old and new Hebrew names, but also all the Aramaic and Greek names that had been sanctified as it were by constant usage. Thus, among the "sacred names" we find Alexander and its abbreviated form Sender; Klonimos and Kalman (from the Greek Kalonymos, "beautiful name"); Gronim (an abbreviated form of Geronymos, "the old man"); and Todros (Jewish version of Theodorus, "God has given"). These names are still used by Jews today, and men are called up to read the Torah by them, so accepted is their Jewish status now.

The Ashkenazic (German, Alsatian, Polish, Austrian, Russian) Jews were more lavish in their use of non-Jewish names for extra-community purposes than any other group. Their Hebrew names, too, were subject to extreme mutations. There are two reasons for this process of corruption: the many different dialects they spoke; and the widespread tendency to confer nicknames and diminutives that were retained in mature years and handed down to the next generation in place of the original Hebrew name, which was often forgotten. Thus the Hebrew name Avraham (Abraham) became Aberke, Aberl, Aberlein, Aberlieb, Aberlin, Aberzuss, Avrom, Afrom, Fromel, Bremel, Ebermann, Ebril. David changed into Tewel, Tewele, and Elchanan into Elkin, Elkan. Eleazar became Lasar, Lazar, Lazarus. Eliezer took on the forms Leeser, Leser, Leyser. Elijah became Elya. Ephraim became Froim, Froikin, Fraime. Ezekiel became Heskel, Hatzkel, and Kaskel. Isaac (Yitzhak) became Eissig, Eisnick, Eisman, Itzig, Gitzok, Hickman, Itzik, Itzl, Zekl, Sickel, Seckel. Israel became Isril, Isserl, Srulik, Srul, Srol. Jacob (Yaakov) became Yekel, Yukel, Yokel, Yankel, Yakobl, Kopel, Kopelman, Yakof, Kofman. Joseph (Yosef) became Yosel, Yosi, Yos, Yesse, Jessel, Jesselman, Joske, Yoske. Judah (Yehuda) became Judel, Udell, Yudke, Yudko. Samuel (Shmuel) became Shmulik, Shmelke, Sanvil, Zavill, Zangwill. Simeon (Shimon) became Shimme, Shimmel, Shimke. Solomon (Shlomo) became Salaman, Salmon, Salmen, Zalman, Zalkin, Zalkind.

The Jewish names which the Ashkenazim adopted in conformity with the rabbinic ordinance were related in a variety of ways to their non-Jewish names:

1. In many cases they were a direct translation into Hebrew of German names. Gottlieb ("beloved of God") became Yedidyah Gottlieb; Bendit (a form of Benedict, "blessed") became Barukh, in its dual form Barukh Bendit. A popular diminutive of the German Gottfried was Gotze; this was corrupted into Goetzl or Getzel, which was translated as Eliakim ("God sustains"), and many Jews were called Eliakim Getz or Getzl. The accommodation between the Jewish world and the outside world had been going on by means of translation for some time. Italian Jews translated Asael ("God has fashioned") for Diofatto, Manoah ("restful") for Tranquillo, and Hayyim ("life") for Vita. French Jews translated Yehiel ("May he live, O god") to Vivant, Hayyim to Vital, and

Mattityahu ("God's gift") to Dieudonné. Greek Jews translated Eliakim ("God sustains") into Anastasios.

2. A second way for inventing Jewish names called into play the skill in casuistry, which Jews had developed in study of the Talmud. In the Bible certain names are found in association with certain terms. For example, Judah is called *gur aryeh*, a lion. A Jew called Loeb ("lion," in German) would therefore adopt as his Hebrew name Judah or Aryeh; this gave him as his full name Judah Layb ("lion," in Yiddish) or Aryeh Layb. Hirsch (which is pronounced Hirz or Herz in the dialects of Upper Germany), "hart," "hind," became Naphtali Herz or Tzvi ("hart," in Hebrew) Hirsch, because the patriarch Jacob in blessing Naphtali calls him a swift-footed hart. A whole variety of names developed out of this form: Hirsch, Herz, Herschel, Herzl, the French Cerf, and the Slavic Jellin, Yellin, Jellinik.

In the same way, Wolff became Benjamin Wolff (Genesis 49:27) and the name forms derived are: Wolf, Wolpe, Wulf, and from the Hebrew Zeev ("wolf") we get Ziff, Zev, Seff, and the Slavic Wilk, Wolk, Walk, the Rumanian Lupo, and the Spanish Lopez.

And because Jacob said to Ephraim (Genesis 48:16) that his seed would multiply as the fish in the sea, the popular German name Fischlin became Ephraim Fischel.

Following Talmudic logic in the interpretation of Genesis 49 the *kinnui* of Issachar should have been the word for donkey. However, this is a derisive term in Europe and is also a reminder of the name of Shechem's father Hamor ("donkey") in the incident of the rape of Dinah (Genesis 34). Never at a loss, the Jews ingeniously substituted the name Baer ("bear"), an animal noted for its strength. (Perhaps it was associated with the idea of *bearing* since the verse reads "and he bowed his shoulder to bear.") Whatever the process, the result was Issachar Ber and the forms Berman, Berko, Berish, etc.

No *kinnui* was developed for Dan because that tribe was

compared with the serpent, and the serpent was, in Jewish tradition, a symbol of evil, the devil, and of death.

3. Finally, similarity of sound with one's non-Jewish name was a sufficient warrant for adopting a sacred name. The French *bon homme* and *bon ami* were popular as a name among the Jews in the form of Bunim. Phonetically it was related to Benjamin; therefore, a German Jew whose *kinnui* was Bunim took Benjamin as his religious name, his name becoming Benjamin Bunim. The Germanic Anselm was adopted in the corrupted form of Anschel and linked with the Hebrew Asher to become Asher Anschel. In some strange way Asher became associated with the *kinnui* Leml, or Lemlin ("lamb"). Asher also appears as Enzlin and as Enzil. Perhaps the latter forms are a mutation of Agnel, the French for "lamb."

In many instances, however, a Hebrew name was con-joined with a non-Jewish name in a purely arbitrary fashion, without any logical or phonetic warrant. But the vast majority of parents selected names for their children because of some phonetic relationship. This relationship in sounds was often given a meaning in popular etymology. This was true in the Biblical and Talmudic eras and it most certainly was true later when Jews no longer spoke Hebrew. Ignorance of the Hebrew name forms often resulted in bizarre creations that, through repeated usage, have continued to this very day. This is particularly true with regard to diminutives. The regular diminutive in medieval French is -*in*, thus giving us Abramin, Itzhakin, Aaronin, Jacobin, Israelin. In southern Germany, where most of the German Jews lived during the Middle Ages, the diminutive -*lin* was used; later on, the diminutive forms were -*le* and -*el*. In North Germany the most common form of the diminutive was -*chen*, and the Jews often used -*che*.

Keeping this in mind, we can follow the development of some interesting name forms: The diminutive of Israel be-came, among French Jews, Israelin, and was pronounced

Isserlin. When the name passed to the German Jews, they heard the diminutive not as the French *-in* but as their own *-lin*. They, therefore, concluded that the name was *Isser*lin. Isser thus became a full-fledged Jewish name among German Jews and even more so among Polish and Lithuanian Jews.

The same process was at work in the case of actual French names. The name Gentille (often written by Jews as Yentille) appears in the diminutive form Yentlin. When that name appeared among German Jews, its French origin was forgotten and the *-lin* was taken as the German diminutive, with the result that the full name became Yente.

Sometimes a French name received a new Jewish form because its original meaning was forgotten. For example, the name Estérine was popular in its diminutive form Térine. In Germany the name appeared as Tríne. The "i" is often changed to "ei" in German (as *Itzhak* became *Eizik*) and so we find Térine (which is already a diminutive) being given additional diminutive forms and becoming Treinel, Treindel, and among Polish Jews Trana, Trandel.

Sometimes the problem was not the lack of knowledge regarding the *form* but an ignorance of the *meaning*. The name Viola, which in French and Italian meant "violet," had in German the forms Veil, Veigelein, and was pronounced Feil, Feigelein. Among Polish Jews the name form was misinterpreted in two ways—it was either understood as Feigel (*feygl*, "bird" in Yiddish), a translation of the Hebrew Tzipporah, or as a diminutive of Feige (*fayg*, "fig," in Yiddish).

Sometimes the Hebrew name was misunderstood because people confused the Hebrew syllable with a German-Yiddish diminutive. A case in point is the development of the combination Menahem Mendel. The *-hem* of Menahem was taken as the *-chen* diminutive of North German. Thus the name appears as Menchen, Menche, Menken, Menke. Among the Jews in southern Germany Menahem was called Menlin,

Menel. This latter form became Mendel in Bavarian and Austrian dialects in which *nl* forms become *ndl* in their pronunciation (Treinel becoming Treindel; Hanna = Hannel and becomes Handel; Gnene = Gnenel and becomes Gnendel). It was assumed, after a while, that the basic form of Menahem had been Mann (*Mann*chen, i.e., the diminutive of "man") and so we find the common combination Menahem Mann or Menahem Mannish.

What happened to Menahem could not be avoided by Mordecai. In areas where *-che* and *-chen* are diminutive forms, Mordecai became Motche and Motke. In areas with other diminutive formations Mordecai appears in the forms Motlin, Motele, Motel, Model, Mukel. What about the letter "r" in Mordecai—what happened to it? Actually the name Mordecai was understood as a German or French name. The name Mord was associated with *mort* ("death" or "corpse," in French) and in German with the word *Mord* ("murder"). The "r" was, therefore, intentionally omitted.

Through a similar misinterpretation the Biblical name Rivke (Rebecca) was read as *Riv* plus the diminutive form *-ke*. Hence we get the form Rivlin for Rebecca, a name that already appears in thirteenth-century Germany.

Yekutiel (Yekusiel) in the abbreviated form Kusiel was understood as a diminutive form of Kus. Kus became Kusmann, which popular etymology associated with Gottesman.

In most instances, however, popular etymology was guided by the sound of the word: Yehiel became Ichel and associated with a rhymed name Michel, resulting in the combination that is still current today—Yechiel Michel.

The rabbinic requirement of a Hebrew name for synagogue purposes was one of the chief factors that preserved the Hebrew character of Jewish men's names; but since women were not called to read the Torah, it is no surprise to discover that medieval feminine names were predominantly non-Jewish. One looks at lists of Jewish women's names and finds the strangest conglomeration of corruptions and diminutives, borrowings and mutations. The names present a weird cacophony of sounds to modern ears, if we are ignorant of their provenance and of the metamorphoses they have undergone. For example: Trestel comes from the German *Troest,* "consolation," and was used for the Hebrew Nehamah, which is also "consolation," as is the Italian name Consolina, which is found only among Jews; Kreindel is from the German *Krone* ("crown"); Breindel derives from the German *braune* ("brunette"); Dvoshke is a corrupted form of Deborah; Tzirel develops from Sarah; Rayzel derives from Rose; Mindel, from Minne, is the diminutive of Wilhelmina.

In all fairness to our forefathers, however, it must be stated that even in the Middle Ages Jews coined new Hebrew names even for their daughters. This was truer of Italian Jews and in Sephardic communities than for Ashkenazim, who allowed accident and circumstance to distort their names beyond all recognition.

A number of Italian and French names that Jews have used are not immediately recognizable because they have been filtered through Yiddish, the language of the large majority of European Ashkenazim. Names brought by Jewish immigrants from one country to another were changed to suit the tastes and fancy of the Jews among whom they settled. In this way, the Jews in Germany took over the names of French and English Jews who fled eastward in the later Middle Ages and settled among them; but they altered both the sounds and spellings. Polish Jews, similarly, "improved" Italian and German names. This went on from one generation to the next until hardly a trace of the original name remained. Thus, it is difficult today to determine the origins of many names. Who would ever guess that Shprinzel is a Polish Jewish "improvement" on Esperanza, brought east by Italian Jews? It was a regular practice for the Jews of Italy to translate the Hebrew

Tikvah ("hope") into Esperanza. The name became Espérance
among the French Jews and was transformed into Sprinze as it
moved through Germany and Poland. Or how discover that
the name Feitel is a German Jewish corruption of the Italian
Vital, itself a translation of the Hebrew Hayyim ("life")? The
popular Yiddish name Zelde is the old German name Salida
("happiness"); Gimpel comes from Gumprecht. The French
name Mince ("tiny," "slender") became Minkche in German-
Yiddish, and the French Célie was transformed into Kele
(Kayla in Yiddish), just as Italian Bella and French Belle
became the Yiddish Bayla.

A number of women's names are names of flowers and
derive from medieval France. Could you ever believe that
poor, banal Yakhne is from Yachent (Jacinthe), i.e., "hya-
cinthe"? The French Fleur ("flower") is still present in Bluma,
though some Blumas were once the Spanish Paloma ("dove").

The name Frohmut ("joy," in German) was a name for the
Hebrew Simhah. In Poland the meaning was forgotten and the
name became Frommet ("pious one") and developed into the
Yiddish woman's name Fruma.

A great deal of confusion surrounds the name Feivus
(Fayvel, in Yiddish). Most commentators on Jewish names
generally relate the name to Phoebus, the ancient Greek god
of light. The poet Heinrich Heine has lent credence to this
assumption by his statement: *Und da heiss er Rabbi Faibisch,
Was auf hochdeutsch heisst Apollo* ("And he is called Rabbi
Faibisch, which is to say Apollo in German").

Dr. Y. G. Gumpertz, of Jerusalem, in a brilliant study, has,
at long last, clarified the subject of the origins of Feivus.
Feivus does not appear with an "F" before the sixteenth
century, and then only in Germany. In older sources it appears
as Vivas, Vives, Vivs, Vivis (in the list of martyrs of 1096 and
1184, in the list of the martyrs of Troyes, and on the
tombstone inscriptions of Frankfurt). From the seventeenth
century the name is spelled sometimes with an "F" and

sometimes with a "V." In Greece, Italy, and Spain the name is found among neither Jews nor Gentiles. In southern France Phoebus is found at times but only in the periods of history when Jews did not reside there. Dr. Gumpertz has shown that the source of the name is the French Vives, Vifs, Vis for the Hebrew Yehiel, Hayyim, and Chai (names connoting "life"). The French forms came into Germany and became Viscl, Fiscl, Feischl, Feis (which was confused with Feist, the German for "fat"), Vivelman, Veivelman, Feibelman, and even Fischman (Fischman having nothing to do with "fish" but deriving from Vis, Visch, and Fisch).

A parallel name for Feivus among Spanish and Italian Jews is Vivanti, Vivant. In Italy and France are also the names Vital and Vidal, which became Feitel in Germany. The female forms for the Hebrew Hayyah and Havah ("life") appear in Spain as Vida and in Greece as Zoe.

The name Feivus (Fayvel, in Yiddish) was bestowed upon a child whose father had died before he was born and whose mother died before his circumcision and naming. The name was a prayer that life be granted to the orphaned child. It was often associated with the name Uri ("light," in Hebrew) or Shraga ("light," in Aramaic) in reference to Proverbs 20:27, "The soul of man is the lamp of God." And the purpose of the name was not only to safeguard the child but to comfort him in his great bereavement. (See Chapter 11 for apotropaic names.)

Thus, Feivish is associated with light but not with Phoebus, the Greek god of light, but rather with the light of life.

These metamorphoses can be recounted by the hundreds. But for every name we can trace back, there are dozens whose origins are lost.

7

From Eizik to Irving: From Shayna to Shirley to Sandra

WE WILL NOW EXAMINE some of the trends that Jewish parents have followed in the past and that they are following today in selecting first names for their children. It is a fact that of the twenty-eight hundred personal names found in the Bible, less than 5 per cent (about 135) are used by Jews today. At first glance this appears strange; and some diehard traditionalists have always decried the fact that the People of the Book make so little use of the names found in it. But to anyone familiar with the history of Jewish name-giving this comes as no surprise.

We have already seen how in the early post-Biblical period foreign names were much more common than Biblical ones. Even during the Talmudic period, in the first five centuries of the Common Era, the number of Aramaic, Greek, and Roman names outnumbered the Biblical ones.

During the Middle Ages, when Jews began to use a secular and a religious name, the secular name became the dominant one in some communities. In some others, an opposite tendency prevailed, perhaps often not so much due to intention as to government insistence on recording Jews by their Jewish names in the community registers. Thus, for example, among the Jews of England, Biblical names were the most popular. Of the 748 names found in the official English records of the twelfth century (the Pipe Rolls) Biblical names are favored: Isaac leads the list with 59; Josce (Joseph), 55; Abraham, 49; Benedict (the Latin form of Barukh), 49; Jacob, 40; and Mosse or Moss (i.e., Moses), 38.

Medieval Christians, for the most part, rejected Old Testament names. Names from the Hebrew Scriptures were borne by Christians not because of any special admiration for Hebrew names but, primarily, because they were names of ancient saints or church fathers. Not till the period of the Reformation did a new attitude toward Biblical names appear among Christians. In the sixteenth and seventeenth centuries, as a reaction against the Roman Catholic church and a new stress on the Bible, Protestant groups highly favored Hebrew names.

In a 1921 study of 100,000 general names, five of the leading fifteen names were Biblical (two from the Old Testament and three from the New Testament). By comparison, a 1929 study of 400,000 general names revealed a total of four Biblical names (one from the Hebrew Scriptures and three from the New Testament). Among Jews, several surveys conducted in the 1940s revealed that of the leading names conferred on Jewish boys in the United States, only two were of Biblical origin. But only one, David, was from the Hebrew Bible. The other, Paul, was a New Testament personage.

A 1942 survey of Jewish names° found only four Biblical names among the leading fifteen names of the new generation and four among the leading fifteen names of the parent generation. The Biblical names of the parent generation were all from the Hebrew Bible: Ruth, Joseph, David, and Samuel. The names of the new generation were Michael, David, Stephen, and Peter. The latter two are from the New Testament. The tendency, today, among Jews is definitely away from Biblical names.

° Reported in Alfred J. Kolatch, *These Are the Names* (New York, 1948).

What relationship is there between the "religious" and the secular name? In the past, two procedures were followed in the selection of the Jewish and secular names. One was the selection of a secular name on the basis of similarity in *sound* with the Hebrew name; the other sought a conformity in *meaning*. As early as the third century B.C.E. we find the phonetic tendency: Menahem becomes Menelaus, Joshua becomes Jason, and Eliakim becomes Alcimus. At the same time Greek and Roman names were selected on the basis of translation: Tuviah becoming Agathon ("good"), Nathaniel becoming Theodotion or Theodorus ("God has given"), and Zadok becoming Justus ("just").

The same procedures were followed through the centuries. In the Middle Ages, on both sides of the English Channel, there was a tendency to translate Hebrew names into French: Hayyim becomes Vives ("life"), Gamliel becomes Dieulecresse ("God increases"), Obadiah becomes Serfdeu ("servant of God"), Jonathan becomes Dieudonné ("gift of God"), and Isaiah becomes Deulesalt ("God saves").

With the onset of the modern emancipation there was an even greater tendency among Jews to imitate the first names current in the general society. Studies of the Jewish community of Berlin at the end of the nineteenth century and the beginning of the twentieth show that the Jews adopted the ordinary first names of their Gentile neighbors but tended to use certain names exceedingly often, so that such names became peculiarly "Jewish." A case in point is the name Isidor, which was used by anti-Semites, especially in Germany, as a derisive nickname for Jews. The notorious Nazi propaganda minister, Paul Josef Goebbels, published in 1931 an anti-Semitic diatribe, *Das Buch Isidor. (The Isidor Book)*

The name Isidor has an interesting history. It means "gift of Isis" in Greek and was adopted by followers of the cult of the Egyptian goddess Isis, who had many votaries in ancient Rome. The name was also fairly common in ancient Greece.

Later, as Christianity began to make converts among the pagans, it became a frequent name among Christians, especially in Spain where it was the name of two saints, Isidore of Seville (sixth and seventh centuries) and Isidore the Ploughman (eleventh or twelfth century). It did not become a "Jewish" name until about the middle of the nineteenth century in Germany, probably because of the great success of a dramatic production *Isidore and Olga*, written by a non-Jew. Jewish parents often gave the name to their sons as a substitute for Isaac (Itzhak) and Yisrael (Israel), but by the twentieth century its popularity waned in favor of such other substitutes for Isaac and Israel as Irving or Ignatz. But as Isidor had become closely identified with Jews in Germany, it was used less and less by non-Jews.

In pre-World War I Germany and in the Austrian monarchy the names Siegfried, Siegbert, Sigismund, and Sigmund also became "Jewish" names and, for that reason, were eventually avoided by non-Jews. Almost all Moritzes were Jews, as well as most of the Ludwigs. Julius was high on the "Jewish" list, too.

A comparable development took place in America with names like Milton and Sidney (a syncopated form for St. Denis) and others which a generation ago became "Jewish" names in the United States because Jews used them so frequently. The name Hymen, derived from Hymen or Hymenaeus, the ancient Greek god of marriage, was another non-Jewish name that became closely associated with Jews in England and America a few generations ago. Among Jewish immigrants, it had become *the* choice for Hayyim.

While French and Italian Jews use both Hebraic and non-Hebraic first names, there appears to be no case where a non-Hebraic name has come to be considered a "Jewish" name.

In the United States, the transition from immigrant generation to first, second, and third generation has been accompanied by constantly changing first name styles. Certain names extremely popular with an earlier generation have subsequently been totally rejected. Very often this rejection was the result of a sensitivity among Jews that such names were excessively identified with immigrant status and with Jewishness.

On the American scene, there was a time when a Jew used a Hebrew name in its English form, such as Solomon or Samuel. They found that the traditional Hebrew or Yiddish forms of a name could not be simply transliterated, because they appeared foreign and outlandish to their non-Jewish neighbors. Today, American Jews follow many of the practices set in motion by our forefathers long ago, such as translation and phonetic assimilation. It has become a common practice, therefore, to give a child an English name because its initial letter is the same as that of his Hebrew name. Thus, a boy who inherits the Hebrew name Abraham could be an Arthur, Avery, or Allen; and a girl named Shayna (or its diminutive Shayndel) could be called Shirley, Sandra, or Susan. Except for the initial letter or sound, there is absolutely no relationship in meaning between the Jewish and the English name.

Styles in name selection continue to change, with every decade or so producing new favorites. Sometimes only a few names survive to be used again in the next generation. At other times a name which has not been used for a number of generations will suddenly become popular and begin to reappear.

When we examine the names used in the various generations we find that the immigrants considered these names desirable: Bessie, Bertha, Clara, Celia, Dora, Etta, Esther, Ethel, Frieda, Fannie, Goldie, Gussie, Ida, Jennie, Lena, Minnie, Mollie, Mary, Nettie, Pearl, Rose, Rebecca (Becky), Sarah, Sadie, Sophie, Tillie, Yetta, and Zelda. And the male names were: Abe, Benjamin, Isadore, Hyman, Sam, Max, Harry, Herman, Irving, Jack, Jacob, Israel, Joseph, Julius, and Louis.

The children of the above were more likely to be called: Alice, Arlene, Beatrice, Bernice, Betty, Blanche, Claire, Doris, Dorothy, Edith, Eileen, Eleanor, Elaine, Evelyn, Florence, Frances, Gertrude, Harriet, Helen, Irene, Jean, Lillian, Lucille, Mildred, Miriam, Muriel, Rhoda, Rosalyn, Selma, Shirley, and Sylvia. And favorite names for boys of the second generation were: Alfred, Arnold, Arthur, Bernard, Charles, Edward, George, Harold, Henry, Herbert, Howard, Jerome, Jules, Lawrence, Leon, Leonard, Martin, Milton, Morton, Norman, Paul, Philip, Ralph, Seymour, Sidney, Stanley, Walter, and William.

The following generation saw the popularization of Ann, Barbara, Beth, Bonnie, Carol, Cheryl, Diane, Ellen, Gail, Jane, Jill, Joan, Joyce, Judy, Karen, Lee, Leslie, Linda, Lois, Lynn, Nancy, Patricia, Roberta, Ronnie, Sandra, Sue, and Susan. And boys' names: Alan, Andrew, Barry, Bruce, Donald, Eric, Gary, Harvey, James, Jay, Jeffrey, Jonathan, John, Kenneth, Lee, Marc, Mark, Michael, Peter, Richard, Robert, Roger, Ronald, Stephen, Steven, and Stuart.

The new arrivals now include Lori, Kim, Cindy, Jennifer, Nicole, Tracey, Stacey, Tammy, Kimberly, Jeri, Lisa, Margo, Marci, Dawn, Robin, Aimee, Brandi, Carrie, Denise, Craig, Scott, Brian, Evan, Keith, Kevin, Matthew, Ross, Shawn, Adam, and Bradley.

In our time the taste in names has become more and more eclectic, and there are few European languages that have not contributed their share. This is especially so in the United States, where the population is drawn from every country in Europe. There was a time when one of the most powerful influences in naming, as in so many other ways, was the movie industry. The names of famous film actors and actresses (frequently fanciful inventions of their own) were freely bestowed on the children of their fans. This accounted for the popularity of such names as Gary and Shirley, Carol, Lana, Maureen, Marlene, Myrna, and Merle.

In recent years the use of more than one given name has become increasingly popular among Jews, just as it was about two centuries ago in Poland. There are several reasons for this development. The widespread practice of naming a child after a deceased relative often poses a problem for parents. They are often faced with several possible choices of names, sometimes with one from the father's side of the family and another from the mother's side. The simplest way out of such a familial dilemma is to resort to the use of two names. In former times, a second impetus to multiple names had also been the practice of giving a "therapeutic name" (see Chapter 11), which became part of the total appellation of the individual and was passed on to another generation.

In the general history of names, Spain was probably the first country to encourage the giving of more than one Christian name, and double given names were used by Spanish noblemen more than nine centuries ago. Germany adopted the custom at the close of the fifteenth century. The custom of using more than one given name became common in England only in the eighteenth century, although a few are found earlier. No one on the *Mayflower* had a middle name. Before the mid-eighteenth century the use of middle names was quite rare in America. Among our first seventeen presidents only three had middle names; but among the last twenty, only three did not have them. In the United States about 75 percent of the male population have middle names, and this has been so for the last century. The use of middle names is increasing, and since Jews follow the popular naming trends, it is safe to assume that Jews will continue to use more than one given name.

While in the United States and England there is no legal restriction on the parents' choice of a name for their children, many European countries do have laws, more or less operative, with the object of regulating names. In France, for example, there is a law dating to 1803 that is still in force and that decrees that names shall be chosen only from those persons known in ancient history or in use in the various religious calendars. Good revolutionaries were averse to using names from the Christian calendar, and so they availed themselves of the permission to use names from ancient history which was interpreted to include a good deal of mythology. Such favorite French names as Marcel, Jules, Aristide, and Achille came into use as a result of this law. The rule is not now very strictly applied, but it still has a restrictive effect. German law forbids using a name that cannot be proven to have been used before. Such regulation, even though it is not rigidly applied, has, on the whole, had the effect of sparing the European countries from the flood of neologisms, which have become part of the name-giving process in the United States and which influence the selection of names by Jewish parents.

8

"And the Cabots Speak Yiddish—by God!"

WHEN THE SPIRIT OF emancipation first began to bestir itself, there were ambivalent feelings among the various European states toward the Jews. Some governments wanted to accelerate the process making Jews an integrated part of the total society. But certain restrictions were also instituted. Joseph II decreed that Austrian Jews adopt family names, and his officials insisted that the names be German, not "Hebrew" or Yiddish. At the same time, Jews were limited to using Biblical first names. Napoleon ordered the Jews in all his territories to assume family names but forbade them to take names based on localities or to adopt the names of famous families. Later, Czarist Russia required Jews to assume family names but restricted the use of certain first names.

The philosophy of Nazi Germany, which totally repudiated the emancipation and rejected any rights for the Jews, expressed itself very directly and clearly in the area of Jewish nomenclature. On August 17, 1938, the Nazi government decreed that Jews could not change their family names. They were even compelled to reassume Jewish names that had been changed. This same law restricted Jews to the use of a limited number of first names. The government specified a list of "official Jewish names," 185 first names for men and 91 for women. The Nazis selected and preferred the eastern European versions of the names instead of the original Biblical forms. Such names as Abraham, David, Joseph, Ruth, and Miriam were not included. Jews already bearing names other than those specified on the list were to assume by January 1, 1939, the additional name of Israel for a male and Sarah for a female. These new names had to be duly registered and faithfully used in all business and legal transactions. This law was finally repealed in September, 1947.

Following their Nazi masters, France, in March, 1942, forbade its Jews to change their family names and Norway, under the Nazi puppet Quisling, forbade its Jews, in July, 1942, to bear Norwegian-sounding names. Thus, the hands on the clock of history and of civilization were turned back.

As Jews entered increasingly into the mainstream of European life, they did not stop with merely adopting family names. The process of *changing* names to suit the taste and style of the western world had become inevitable. This process has been especially evident in the United States, where there has been a continuing tendency to Americanize Jewish names encouraged by a variety of factors, not the least of which is the comparative legal ease by which one can change his name in the United States. There are very few restrictions on assuming a new name. One has merely to file an application with a court of record. Unless there appears some real grounds for a denial (such as intent to defraud or invasion of the rights of another), the application is usually granted.

Another factor that changed names of American Jews was the "improvement" that many immigration officials made upon names of immigrants. These officials sometimes caught just a snatch of a long German or Slavic name and simply recorded what they thought they heard or what they felt they could spell out on their forms. Many American Jewish family names today are the product of the confrontation of a puzzled official and a bewildered immigrant. The result is a bizarre assortment of new and misinterpreted names. Sometimes, the answers given by Jews (and the same was true in the case of other immigrants) to the questions of officials were turned into surnames. Thus, a Jew who stated in Yiddish that his name was *poshet Yankel* ("simply Yankel") was registered as Yankel Poshet, while a family who exclaimed in Hebrew *anu lo nayda* ("we don't know") had the name Neuda entered.

The desire on the part of newcomers or their children to become completely assimilated and totally integrated into American society motivated many to consciously and intentionally modify, shorten, translate, or change cumbersome foreign-sounding names into short, simple American-sounding ones. Of the various groups of immigrants to this country, some clung more tenaciously to their awkward-sounding names than others. The Poles and the Czechs (e.g., Przybyszewski and Hrdlicka are two names still prominent in the Chicago telephone directory) probably hold first place in their heroic attempt to preserve onomastic continuity, with the Hungarians, the Greeks, and the Italians not too far behind. The Irish and the Germans have always felt at home with their names, which are so common as to constitute a segment of the majority name group. Still, even among these ethnic groups, there have been quite a number who, by means of a slight change of a consonant or vowel, have concealed their origin.

In the process of name changing Jews appear to have shown greater activity and ingenuity than other ethnic groups. Perhaps it is the general tendency of upward social mobility that has been a characteristic of Jewish life in America. Or it may be a special sensitivity and awareness among Jews that as a minority they have suffered much discrimination. We shall later attempt to analyze some of the possible causes that motivate Jews to modify their names. But the fact is quite evident that many in America do not like their names or, at least, do not feel comfortable with them.

Statistics are not easy to come by, but there are rough statistics that indicate that about fifty thousand Americans a year apply to state courts to change their family names. Of these, about 80 per cent are Jews. If we estimate about four persons to a family, this means that about 160,000 Jews shed or modify their cognomens annually.

State courts rarely reject an application for a change of name. An applicant usually attests that his name is burdensome and the cause of hardship. His application is submitted to a judge, who almost never asks to see the applicant, and the relief is granted. In reality, only a very small percentage of such applications are based on obvious or actual hardship. The relatives of a wholesale murderer, for example, may request and be granted permission to change their name. One can also appreciate why many people named Hitler felt it necessary to change their names. With Jews, and other minority groups, the matter is more complex.

Of the various waves of Jewish immigration to America, the Sephardic Jews steadfastly stuck to their traditional Spanish and Portuguese names (Lopez, Touro, Seixas). German Jews were also proud of their names, although sometimes a letter or umlaut would be dropped in order to facilitate spelling and pronunciation. Thus, Rebecca Gratz, the prototype of *Ivanhoe*'s Rebecca, was really a Graetz, and the name Filene was originally Filehne. When the large wave of German Jews began to arrive in America in the middle of the nineteenth century—settling in New York, Philadelphia, Cincinnati, St. Louis, and all over the West and South—the struggling peddlers (who subsequently became the merchant princes) felt no need to conceal their origin by a change of name. In the first place, their religion would have defeated the purpose of such protective coloration. Nor was there a sense of onomastic difference on their part, since in many of the communities in which they settled there were many Gentiles with similar names. And when the families eventually gained prominence in the commercial or industrial field, there was no longer any need for the Bernheims or Guggenheims to assume a different name.

The British Jews (the Isaacses, Jacobses, Nathans, Samuelses, etc.) never showed any leanings toward sailing under false colors, and they had nothing to be sorry for in this respect. An Isaacs not only became Lord Chief Justice of England but attained the rank of viceroy of India; while another Isaacs became the first nonroyal governor-general of Australia. In America, too, a Ribicoff, a Javitz, a Goldberg, and a Greenspan, and many others have been able to move to the top rungs of politics and government service.

As hundreds of thousands of Jews began to pour into the United States from eastern Europe in the 1880s, Jewish names in America took on a different cast. A great many of the names were, to be sure, Germanic, partly because of German provenance but mainly through the Yiddish background. And many of the name forms were Slavic, like those ending in -ski, -ev, -off, -vitch, -wicz, -in, etc.

Generally speaking, the first generation of the new immigrants was willing to abide with the names it brought from the old country. Only among the most practical did the thought occur of Americanizing their names. Sometimes a minute change would spell the difference between a foreigner and a native.

Almost half of the Jews who change their names in America each year are content with shortening: Greenberg, to Green or Greene; Itzkovitz to Itts; Mayefsky to May; Rushnevsky to Rush; Kaminetzky to Kamin or Kamins; Weisberg to Weiss; Ewigkeit to Ewig; Pearlman to Pearle; Bassovsky to Bass; Rabinowitz to Rabin or Rabb; Rosenberg to Rose; Rosenblatt to Rosen; Rubinstein to Rubin; Udelevsky to Udell; Targownik to Targ or Tarr; Targovetsky to Targow; Kempenich to Kemp; Malawsky to Mall; Elowitz to Elow; Gluckenspiegel to Gluck; Savitzky to Savit; or Zaretsky to

Zaret. The shorter name is easier to spell over the phone and fits quite comfortably on any dotted line. But one suspects conformity, too; after all, Hollingsworth, Throckmorton, and O'Shaughnessy do not seem so ready to delete a syllable from their names.

What of the almost 60 per cent who go in for more drastic alterations, who change Epstein to Eaton, Goldstein to Garrett, Glenbocki to Glenn, Hamburger to Harlow, Fastenburg to Forster, Portnoy to Portes, Shapotkin to Shay, Bolotsky to Bell, Kanevsky to Kane, Cohn to Cole, or Collins, Finkelstein to Fields or Finch, Prensky to Prentiss, Abramson to Ranson, Rosenthal to Ronall, Rappaport to Rose, Rosenzweig to Ross, Turetzky to Tresley, Wisotsky to Vernon, Deutch to Dorian, Lenchitzky to Lance, Lazarowitch to Layton, Lifshitz to Leaf, Levenson to Lenson, Mendelson to March, and Markowitz to March, Marsh, or Martin; Cherkasky to Chase, Lowenbraun to Lowell, Levy to Lyndon, Sudnovsky to Summers, Yablunsky to Yale, Himmelfarb to Howard, Jurnove to James, Jerusalimsky to Jerison, Weisberger to Weston, Zamattison to Madison, Goldberg to Gorman, or Weintraub to Winthrop?

The above transformations preserve the initial letter or sound of the original name. But a Levine may also become a Roberts and a Schwartz a Lawrence or a Grushevsky a Ludwig or a Tennenbaum a Stone. Whether they choose a fancy name or a flat name it is an odd kind of thing to do in America. It is understandable in xenophobic France or in homogeneous England that someone with an outlandish name should want to lose his "foreignness." But in the polyglot United States alien names, like alien origins, are almost as much the rule as the exception, as a glance at the telephone book, a list of the honored war dead, names on a good football team, or a list of contributors to the Red Cross will show.

But apparently many Jews have found such considerations of little weight, as a look at the record shows: Half the Jews in

the U.S. Armed Forces during World War II bore last names
that were not recognizably Jewish, according to the records of
the American Jewish Historical Society. To Jewish chaplains it
was a commonplace for Private Jones or Corporal Kingsford
or Sergeant Vernon to help in the distribution of *yarmulkes*
before services, and it was routine for them to write home to
Mama and Papa Winston when son Louis was killed or
wounded in action. A member of the Graves Registration
Command relates: "We soon became accustomed to placing
Stars of David over graves of GI's with an 'H' on their dog-tags
but with the most un-Jewish names you can imagine."

Often the changed name loses its distinction when too
many co-religionists use it. Levin, a Russian name (cf. *Anna
Karénina* by Leo Tolstoy), can be seen as an illustration.
Russian Jews were quick to note the easy transition from Levi
or Levy to Levin. Soon there were so many Jews using the
name that every Levin or Lewin was taken for a Jew. But the
name was then given a French twist, in Le Vine, La Vine,
Levigne, and even Lhévinne. Similarly, Lebovich was often
changed to Lebow and Lebow itself, gallicized into Lebeau.

Another process developed that was especially suited for
changing Jewish names derived from places of origin, voca-
tions, or personal characteristics. This was the process of
translation. Schneider, when not changed to Snyder, becomes
Taylor; Chazin becomes Cantor; Schwartz turns into Black
and Weiss is translated into White; Greenstein becomes
Greenstone, Greenberg becomes Greenhill, and Greenblatt is
changed to Greenleaf; Routenstein becomes Redstone;
Schoenkind becomes Fairchild. Many names are so similar in
sound that the translation shows but a slight deviation: Gold,
Brown, Tucker, Silver, Binder, Flaxman, Cooper, Houseman,
Singer, Long, Locker, Fiedler, Goodman, Fisher, Factor
(originally meaning "agent"), and many others. The translated
name sometimes offers less of an objection on the principle
that the *spirit* of the family trade-mark is still there, although
the sound is the *motive*.

The trend in name changing has also gone beyond translation, abbreviation, or assonance. Typical American names are frequently chosen without any relationship to the original name. There was a time when the use of Gentile names was thought to stem from a feeling of inferiority and insecurity and as the mark of one who was attempting to abandon all ties with his Jewish past. This is no longer true. A number of these typically American names (Clark, Grant, Warren, Perry, Palmer, Ross, Webster, Ford, Spencer, Foster, Nelson, Lincoln, Wilson, Swift, Douglas, Gilbert, etc.) crop up in Jewish organizations, even in the Yiddish press. Hebrew teachers and rabbis are their bearers, also.

There comes to mind the tale (perhaps apocryphal) of a New England Jewish family by the name of Kabakoff who petitioned to have their name changed to Cabot. After some initial difficulty, the court sustained the petition and the Kabakoffs officially became Cabots—whereupon the wags reported:

> And this is good old Boston
> The home of the bean and the cod,
> Where the Lowells speak only to Cabots
> And the Cabots speak Yiddish—by God!

What prompts the intentional change of name? Commercialism, social aspirations, conformism, convenience, escapism? One study reveals that the choice of a distinctly Gentile name seemed evidence that there was some impulse toward concealment of Jewishness. In a number of cases, parents changed the family name to help their children get into medical school. A number of individuals stated that the purpose of changing their name was to overcome anti-Semitism (real or imagined). Some hoped for social advantage; others thought they could advance higher in their professions. The results of several investigations as to the reasons for changing names may be summarized as follows: name changing is an attempt of the individual to integrate with society. Three principal reasons can be observed—a desire to eliminate a difficult name that differs from the general linguistic pattern; a desire to hide one's ethnic and religious background; or a desire to avoid a name which has unpleasant connotations, evokes ridicule, etc.

Is it right to change one's family name? Some Jewish writers have approved while others have vigorously denounced those who change their names. The critics deplore what they consider the sacrifice of one's heritage and the surrender to prejudice; at the same time they also deny the effectiveness of name changing. These observations raise important ethical questions that deserve detailed study, but that are outside the scope of this book.

An editorial that appeared in *Aufbau*, a newspaper established to help German-speaking Jewish refugees become more integrated in the United States, while approving the principle of name changing, cautioned as follows:

> Many of the Jewish immigrants who came here in recent years also changed their names, the new name usually containing an echo of the original surname. Of course, there is no reason to change strictly Jewish names, for they are generally known and respected. But there can be no objection if Jews starting a new life try to drop names which arrogant anti-Semitic officials in Europe at one time pinned on their forefathers.

> As a matter of fact, in the United States a sensible change of name is regarded favorably as an external symptom of assimilation. The emphasis is on the word "sensible." The choice of a name demands tact. Only very naive and tactless persons go to extremes when they select a name. Immigrants who take names that are virtually the hereditary property of old families display the characteristics of the *nouveau riche* and of psychological insecurity. It is simply not done to adopt all of a sudden some such name as Wilson, Blaire, Biddle,

Jefferson, Revere, Cummings, Lincoln, or Washington. Not only does the choice of such a name excite ill feeling; it also invites scorn and derision. And ultimately the mocking of the community defeats what had originally been a sensible intention. A person who decides to change his name should be guided by three principles: moderation, tact, and unobtrusiveness.

We come now to the dénouement. Does name changing always bring good fortune? Does it spell happiness for the individual who has thus adjusted himself? While in a number of instances the change can help in the attainment of some social goal, in many other cases it can occasion problems that had not been dreamed of. Perhaps subsequent generations will reap the benefits, but the recently transformed are often shunned by their relatives and friends. They are the butt of snide remarks and stinging humor. There are also guilt feelings present, for in a sense there is a severance of father-son continuity, and the question of identity must recur over and over again in the mind of the sensitive who, seeking to adjust themselves to society, have only betrayed their maladjustment.

Somehow one finds himself thinking of the joke about a George Stanislaukas who asked for permission to change his name to Sprague. Some twenty years later, Sprague petitioned the court to be allowed to change his name back to Stanislaukas. When the judge asked him why, he said his friends made fun of him, persisted in calling him Stanislaukas, and simply couldn't pronounce Sprague.

Interestingly, it is not the third-generation Jews (children of American-born parents), as one might suppose, who go for name changing. A survey of a number of universities where there are large enrollments of Jewish students revealed that no more than a handful of Jewish students inform the registrars of changes of name. Name changing is practiced mainly by Jews now over thirty, mostly the children of immigrants.

This fact seems to support the theory developed by Marcus Hansen, a sociologist who studied the behavior patterns of Scandinavian immigrants to America. Hansen discovered that the children of immigrants usually tend to reject their parents' ethnic behavior patterns. In their effort to adjust to new surroundings the members of the second generation slough off everything which is foreign and likely to prove an obstacle. Their children, however, the third generation, already quite secure in their Americanism, are receptive to their grandparents' cultural and religious patterns. Thus, concluded Hansen, it would seem that what the sons of immigrants wish to forget, the grandchildren wish to remember.

It may well be that the new emphasis on ethnicity and the abandonment of the traditional melting-pot concept will become operative among the younger generation of Jews in their attitude toward changing their family names.

9

Shalom, Nimrod!
Welcome back, Hagar!

A NEW TENDENCY in the selection of first names and surnames was generated by the rise of Zionism and the revival of the Hebrew language, which marked the Jewish national rebirth toward the end of the nineteenth century and became even more intense during the twentieth century. This new interest resulted in the establishment of a Commission for Hebrew Nomenclature *(Vaad Shemon Ivri)*, originally a part of the Jewish Agency and now a division of Israel's Ministry of the Interior, and in the compilation of a multivolume *Shemon Ivri* (List of Hebrew Names), containing both rules for the Hebraization of non-Jewish names and a great deal of information on specific Hebrew names.

Within the *yishuv* (the Jewish community of Palestine before May, 1948) and, subsequently, in the State of Israel there have been numerous styles of first names, reflecting differences of origin and of generation. To a certain extent each of the various elements that have been woven together to create the present Israeli society has retained its own traditional nomenclature. Thus, among the Hasidim and among the Yemenites and, generally, among the more traditional families there is a tendency to be more conservative in the use of old, established Hebrew names and customs of naming. However, successive generations of native-born Israelis have tended to reject the older naming patterns and fashions. They have created their own styles, sometimes utilizing obscure Biblical names, at other times incorporating ancient Canaanite (Moabite, Edomite, etc.) names, and the nomenclature of the pre-Patriarchal era and even making use of antediluvian nomenclature. They also very often fashion wholly new designations.

To a limited degree this return to the use of Hebrew first names has carried over into Western Jewish communities. Thus, while the predominant tendency of Jews in America, as we have seen above, has been to follow the naming style of the majority culture around them, some of the newly created Israeli names have found their way among American Jews, especially for those who have embraced Zionism and Hebrew culture. It is not unusual to come across a Tamar, Gilah, Renah, Avivah, Shirah, Adinah, or Ari in the schools of Boston, New York, Philadelphia, Denver, or Los Angeles.

In Israel, names are devised or changed according to certain established procedures:

1. The elimination of Diaspora influences and admixtures. Jewish names are purged of all the "foreign" accretions. A Hebrew component, if missing, is restored; if present, it is left standing alone. Thus, Mendel disappears, and Menahem remains; Getzel is dropped, and Eliakim is reinstated. Judeo-Polish Zlate and German Golde (the English Goldie) are translated either to a simple Hebrew Zehavah or to a fancier Zehavit and Zehuvah. Frayda is translated into Alizah, Hedvah, Ditzah, Gilah, or Renah, all of which contain the same "joy." Gittel becomes Tovah ("good"); Hinda ("doe") becomes Ayalah or Ayelet; Liba becomes Ahuvah ("love"), Pearl and Perl become Margalit or Marganit; Rose and Rayzel become Vardah, Vered, Vardina, or Vardit; and Shayndel ("beauty") is translated into Yaffah.

2. Some women's names can be simply made of men's names with the addition of a feminine ending: Ariellah/Ariel;

Binyaminah/Binyamin; Davidah/David; Daniellah/Daniel; Eytanah/Eytan; Gabriellah/Gabriel; Gidonah/Gideon; Yisraelah/Yisrael; Josephah/Joseph; Meirah/Meir; Odedah/Oded; Shimonah/Shimon; Sinayah/Sinai.

3. The Bible and other Hebrew literary works become the sources for names of children. An examination of the family records of hundreds of Israelis indicates that the following provided the most popular for boys:

Adin, one of the exiles returning from Babylon (Ezra 2:15);

Amitai, father of Jonah (2 Kings 14:25);

Amnon, first-born of David (2 Samuel 3:2);

Alon, son of Shimon (1 Chronicles 4:37);

Asaf, a Levite (1 Chronicles 6:24);

Asa, king of Judah (1 Kings 15:9);

Aviezri, (Judges 6:11);

Avishai, one of King David's commanders (1 Samuel 26:6);

Adar, grandson of Benjamin (1 Chronicles 8:3);

Ariel, a leader in the time of Ezra (Ezra 8:6);

Amos;

Avner, commander of Saul's army (1 Samuel 17:55);

Azgad, head of a family of exiles from Babylon (Ezra 2:12);

Aylon, a Judge (Judges 12:11);

Ehud, a Judge (Judges 3:15);

Elad, an Ephraimite (1 Chronicles 7:21);

Elitzur, prince of the tribe of Reuben (Numbers 1:5);

Eytan, a wise man (1 Kings 5:11) or a Levite (1 Chronicles 6:27);

Eran, an Ephraimite (Numbers 26:36);

Gad, name of one of the twelve tribes;

Gideon, a Judge (Judges 6:27);

Gadi, one of the twelve scouts sent by Moses to explore the Holy Land (Numbers 13:11);

Gilead, father of Jephthah (Judges 11:1);

Iftah, a Judge (Judges 11:1);

Iddo, head of the Temple servants (Ezra 8:17);

Itzhar, grandson of Levi (Exodus 6:21);

Matan, in the time of Jeremiah (Jeremiah 38:1);

Oded, a prophet in the time of King Ahaz (2 Chronicles 28:9);

Omri, king of Israel who built Samaria but "who did evil in the sight of the Lord" (1 Kings 16:21);

Ram, one of David's ancestors (Ruth 4:19);

Uzi, one of the exiles from Babylon (Ezra 7:4);

Yoav, commander of David's army (1 Samuel 26:6);

Yoram, king of Judah;

Yigal, one of the scouts sent by Moses (Numbers 13:7);

Yariv, one of the leaders of the exiles from Babylon (Ezra 8:16);

Yakhin, son of Shimon (Genesis 46:10);

Yehoiakhin, king of Judah (2 Kings 24:6);

Zerubavel, governor of the community of Judea in the period of the return (Haggai 1:1).

Among the most popular Biblical names for girls are the following:

Abishag, "companion" of David (1 Kings 1:3);

Avital, wife of David (2 Samuel 3:4);

Bilhah, concubine of Jacob (Genesis 29:29);

Hagit, wife of David (2 Samuel 3:4);

Hamutal, wife of King Josiah (2 Kings 23:3);

Ephrat, wife of Caleb (1 Chronicles 2:19);

Hulda, a prophetess (2 Kings 22:14);

Michal, daughter of Saul and wife of David (1 Samuel 14:49);

Pua, an Egyptian midwife (Exodus 1:15);

Shlomit, daughter of Zerubavel (1 Chronicles 3:19);

Tamar, daugher-in-law of Judah (Genesis 38:7) or daughter of David and Absalom's sister (2 Samuel 13:1);

Tirzah (Numbers 26:33);

Yael (Judges 4:17).

Some interesting facts come to light when we examine

these Biblical names. First of all, there is a strong identification on the part of many in Israel today with the return from
the Exile that took place in the time of Ezra. The new *Shivat
Tziyon* (Return of Zion) often expressed itself by using the
names of the Biblical books of the first period of restoration
(Ezra and Chronicles). Secondly, the names, for the most part,
are of leaders, prophets, kings, members of the royal family,
generals, Judges (in the Biblical meaning of rulers)—all having
played some historic role in the building or rebuilding of the
land. But there is also a preference for any Biblical name pre-
or post-Patriarchal, of Hebrew or pagan origin.

Sometimes a name is selected without any heed to whether
it was borne by the righteous or the wicked. We find in Israel
today the name Aviram, also the name of one of the
ringleaders in the rebellion against Moses (Numbers 16:1) and
whom the earth swallowed up. Perhaps the parents who
selected this name had in mind another Aviram, one of the
builders of Jericho (1 Kings 16:34). Tzipor, the father of Balak
(Numbers 22:2), who hired Balaam to curse Israel; and
Ataliah, daughter of Jezebel and the most wicked queen of
Judah (2 Kings 8:26); and Shimrit, a Moabite (2 Chronicles
24:26); and Reuma, a concubine of Abraham's brother Nahor
(Genesis 22:24); and Delilah, Samson's concubine (Judges
16:4); and Hagar, the mother of Ishmael, who was always
looked upon as outside the Hebraic fold and tradition—all are
present in modern Israel.

There has been, for a long time, an accepted practice
among Jews not to give children names of Biblical personages
who lived before Abraham. In the entire Talmudic literature,
the sole exception to this practice is the name Mahalalel
(Genesis 5:13). During the Middle Ages, other exceptions were
Hava (Eve), Noah, and Hanoch (Enoch) (see later, Chapter
11). The contemporary Israelis, however, are not too concerned about this, since among the most popular names today
are Ada, the wife of Lamech (Genesis 4:19); Peleg, the son of
Ever (Genesis 10:25); and Yuval, Ada and Lamech's son and

the inventor of musical instruments (Genesis 4:21). But the greatest surprise is the popularity of the name Nimrod (Genesis 10:8), who is depicted in rabbinic literature as Abraham's chief adversary, as an idolater who inculcated the disbelief in God, as one of the seven most notorious sinners in the world, and as one of the five most wicked individuals in the history of mankind. Small wonder that several *mohalim* (ritual circumcisors) in Israel recently petitioned the rabbinate for guidance to resolve their dilemma when officiating at a ceremony in which the boy is to be given the name Nimrod. They declared that they found the name troubling to their conscience and deemed it a profanation of the Covenant of Abraham, the *brith*. Several suggestions were offered by the rabbis. One was for the *mohel* to leave after the circumcision and not participate in the naming ritual which follows. A second suggestion was that perhaps there should be two names given to a Jewish child—as it has been done by Jews outside Israel living in a Gentile environment for centuries—one, a *religious* Hebrew name and the second a *secular* Hebrew name.

In the Israeli search for Biblical names there are some other interesting innovations occurring. The names of places are becoming first names: Gilboa (a mountain), Arnon (a wadi), Givon (a city), and Geva (a city) have become masculine names. Dimona (a city), Kinereth (a sea), Eilat (a city), Carmela (a mountain), and Galila (a district) are popular feminine names.

A number of currently popular feminine names originally served as masculine names: Anat, originally was the father of Shamgar, a Judge (Judges 3:31), though also the name of a Canaanite goddess; Aya, the name of an Edomite male (Genesis 36:24); Dikla, the grandson of Ever (Genesis 10:27); Levana (Ezra 2:45); Noga, a son of David (1 Chronicles 3:7); Ofra, a man from the tribe of Judah (1 Chronicles 4:14); Tikvah, father-in-law of Hulda the Prophetess (2 Kings 22:14);

Yona, the Hebrew for the Yiddish Teybel and the German Taube ("dove"), but in the Bible it is the name of a man; and Zmira, a Benjamite (1 Chronicles 7:8).

4. From the post-Biblical period we have the name Maccabi, in honor of Judah Maccabeus, who led the Hasmonean Revolt. Giora and Bar-Kokhba are names from the Talmudic period which are enjoying popularity in Israel today. Simon bar Giora was one of the central figures in the revolt against Rome (66–70 c.e.) and the charismatic military commander of Jerusalem when the city fell. Bar-Kokhba was the messianic and legendary figure around whom the people rallied in the revolt of 132 c.e.

5. New names are being constantly created in Israel in every walk of life. Even the names of things and objects are made use of. Many of the new names express the sentiments, hopes, and impulses of a people restored to the land of their forefathers. The field of creativity is a vast one. The only criteria are euphony, simplicity, and brevity, although sometimes these appear to be sacrificed for originality. Some of these names are associated with the Zionist experience—names like Or-Tzion ("light of Zion"), Yehi-Am ("may the people live"), Yehi-Shalom ("may peace live on"), Balfur (in tribute to Arthur James Balfour and the Balfour Declaration), Bilu (an acronym for b*et yaakov lekhu venelkha,* "House of Jacob, come and let us go" [Isaiah 2:5], the name of the first group of Russian Jewish student settlers in Palestine in 1882), and Tzahal (which means "joy" but is associated with the Israel Defense Forces whose acronym is Tzahal, T*zvah Haganah Leyisrael).* All these are masculine names.

And for girls there are invented names, too: Herzlia (in honor of Theodore Herzl), Aliyah (wave of immigration), Tziyonah (feminine of Zion), Tehiya ("revival," "renaissance"), Balfura, and Nili (an acronym for n*etzah yisrael lo yeshaker,* "the strength of Israel will not lie" [1 Samuel 15:29], the name of the Jewish secret intelligence organization that

carried on pro-British spying operations during World War I
in Syria and Palestine, then under Turkish rule).

Among the many new Hebrew first names that have been
introduced in Israel are the following for girls:

Avivah ("spring")

Avivit ("lilac")

Azah ("strong,"
"bright,")

Bat-Ami
("daughter of my
people")

Dafne ("Laurel")

Daliah ("Dahlia")

Dalit ("trailing
vine")

Dorit ("of this
era")

Emunah ("faith")

Eliraz ("my God is
a mystery")

Eliorah ("my God
is light")

Galiah ("wave")

Geulah
("redemption")

Hadarah
("splendid")

Hemdah ("desire")

Hillah ("halo")

Ilanah ("tree")

Irit ("daffodil")

Ivriyah ("Hebrew")

Leorah ("light to
me")

Mirit ("sweet
wine")

Neimah
("pleasant")

Nitzah ("a bud")

Nitzhiya
("eternal")

Nurit ("buttercup")

Netivah ("path")

Nirit ("caraway,"
"ploughed field")

Navah ("beautiful")

Netah ("plant")

Ohelah ("tent")

Ornah ("pine")

Orah ("light")

Orit ("radium")

Oshrat
("fortunate")

Rimonah
("pomegranate")

Ramah ("high")

Rananah ("fresh")

Roni ("song")

Ronit ("song")

Segulah
("treasure")

Sigliah ("violet")

Simonah
("notation")

Sivanah ("of the
month of Sivan")

Taliah ("lamkin")

Talmah ("furrow")

Temirah ("tall,"
"erect," like a
palm)

Tzelilah ("clear")

Tzuriah
("steadfast")

Tzafrirah
("morning
zephyr")

Yoninah ("little
dove")

Zivah ("radiant")

And for boys:

Adiv ("courteous," "polite")
Amir ("tree-top")
Ari (an abbreviation for Aryeh but popular as a full name)
Amiram ("my people is lofty")
Doron ("gift")
Dror ("freedom")
Dror-Li ("my freedom")
Eyal ("stag")
El-Ami ("my people's")
Gal ("wave")

Gozal ("gosling")
Gil ("joy")
Gili ("my joy")
Gur ("cub")
Gaalyahu ("God has redeemed")
Ilan ("tree")
Nir ("furrow")
Nitzan ("bud")
Noam ("delight")
Narkis ("narcissus")
Ofer ("young hart")
Omer ("sheaf," of grain)
Oran ("pine")
Orli ("my light")
Ron ("sing")

Ronen ("sing")
Shai (a nickname for Shaya, the Yiddish diminutive of Isaiah but popular in this form which . means "gift" in Hebrew)
Tal ("dew")
Yagil ("he will rejoice")
Zohar ("brightness," "glow")

6. Not all Israeli names are selected according to the styles described above. Some people have refused to give up their non-Hebrew first names. This may be due to a variety of reasons: they may have come to Israel as adults with firm names or may have established themselves with non-Hebrew names (even Golda Meir has kept her Yiddish first name); others found the language barrier too difficult to overcome (there are still neighborhoods in Jerusalem, Tel Aviv, and Nehariyah where one hears Yiddish, English, German, or Hungarian); and others may just not have felt comfortable with a new name (perhaps they could not identify the family patriarch, Uncle Isidor, with Uzi). And so, an accommodation was worked out whereby the non-Hebrew name appears in a Hebrew transliteration—such names as Bluma, Golda, Harry, and Isidor.

10

"Who Was Who?"

IF FAMILY NAME CHANGING among Jews in America has become significant of late, Jewish surnames in Israel have undergone a veritable revolution. Israelis have Hebraized their names at a feverish rate, as though the taking on of a new name were an act of spiritual rebirth. In a series of articles that appeared in the Hebrew monthly *Bitzaron*, the late Dr. Mordecai Kosover pointed out that the practice of Hebraizing family names began sporadically among the early *halutzim*. It was in the early period, back in 1879, that Eliezer Perlman, the great lexicographer, became Ben Yehudah.

The Second Aliyah, which was motivated by the Kishinev pogroms, and the abortive First Russian Revolution of 1905, brought to Palestine a number of young Russian Jews—among them David Green and Isaac Shimshelevich—who became in Palestine, Ben Gurion and Ben-Zvi. Another early immigrant, Shmuel Czaczkes, is perhaps better known to us today as S. J. Agnon, the Israeli Nobel Prize laureate. Ben Gurion and Ben-Zvi probably changed their names not altogether as the result of Jewish nationalism but, also, in order to function in a secret Zionist organization under the oppressive Czarist regime. One wonders whether they would have changed their names after their reaching important office. While it is true that Ben-

Zvi's successor to the presidency of Israel, Shazar, was formerly *Sh*nayer Zalman *R*ubashov and the present incumbent in the office, Katzir, came from Russia as Katchalski, it is also a fact that the first president of Israel, the renowned Haim Weizmann never changed his family name. It is reported that on one occasion someone mildly reproached him for not picking a pure Hebrew name, and Weizmann smiled and replied with his typical Yiddish humor, *di tsore iz, ikh hob shoyn a nomen,* "the trouble is that I already have a name" (meaning a reputation).

After a slow start, name changing was stepped up considerably under the British mandate as a result of pressure from Zionist leaders who wished to give Palestine a "Hebrew appearance." Another factor was the adoption of secret names (a *nom de guerre*) by members of the Jewish underground organizations, during the British mandate. With the achievement of independence these names were retained. Later, the process of name changing permeated the Israeli army, the core of whose officers was recruited from former Haganah members. Even while Israel's War of Independence was still on, a pamphlet was circulated among members of the Israeli soldiers calling upon them to discard their foreign names and choose Hebrew names.

The establishment of the State of Israel gave a tremendous impetus to Hebraizing names. In the first year of independence, seventeen thousand men and women changed to Hebrew names. The rush was so great that the Department of Immigration had to establish a special office for the purpose of speeding up the legal machinery. Sometimes parents changed their name to one already selected by a son or daughter in the army. Often, the name selected was the end product of much research and the result of consultation and imput by all members of a family. Some specialists in philology and phonetics even offered their services to suggest an expertly devised name—for a fee. (One cannot help but recall the time

a century and a half earlier when Jews were *forced* to pay
money to German and Austrian government officials for the
privilege of obtaining a fine-sounding name.)

Many of the government and community leaders climbed
on the bandwagon in this remarkable reverse process of
forming Jewish names. Moshe Shertok became Sharett; Rabbi
Meir Berlin became Bar-Ilan; Elath was derived from Epstein;
Dr. Avraham Granot, head of the Jewish National Fund,
created his name from Granovsky. Not only did the *Palestine
Post* become the *Jerusalem Post* but its editor, Gershon
Agronsky, became Agron. Israel's ambassador to Argentina at
that time, Yaakov Tchernowitz became Tzur and Levi
Shkolnik, treasurer of the Jewish Agency, became Eshkol. The
first member of the Knesset to change his name was Yisrael
Idelson, and the occasion took everyone by surprise. In the
morning session, he conducted all his legislative affairs as
Idelson, but in the evening session as he took his place at the
Knesset rostrum to participate in the debate, he was recognized by the Speaker as Mr. Bar-Yehuda, and for a moment his
colleagues could not associate the name with the face.

Of course, not all changes of names were so dramatic or
instantaneous. Golda Myerson, for whatever reasons, refused
to be rushed into any change of name. It was not until 1956,
when she was appointed foreign minister, that she changed
her name to Meir. (Israel's foreign ministry requires that
anyone serving outside of Israel have a Hebrew name.)

Official announcements regularly appeared in the news-
papers listing the former name and the new name, and this
was the only legal formality required. It became so that wags
would say that while in the United States the biographical
dictionary of outstanding Americans is called *Who's Who?*—in
Israel such a book should be called "Who *Was* Who?" and
that when two Jews meet in Israel, the proper way for an
introduction is: "My name *was* Feldman. What was yours?"

Still, the new and revolutionary process was not without

its dissenters. Hundreds of articles have been published stating the pros and cons of Hebraizing European surnames. Some complained about the lack of a systematic method in transforming European names into Hebrew ones. Others argued that, for reasons of sentiment, the old names should not be given up, and some Israelis, particularly those with some firsthand experience of the Holocaust, have resisted the trend to rid all names of Diaspora influence, feeling that the perpetuation of the old names is a way of keeping the memory of a cherished past alive. Others have wondered whether the Hebraization of a family name in Israel would not create further barriers between the State and the Jewish communities outside it.

Finally, some have wondered whether it is fair for citizens to be "pressured" into such a process. And while it is true that no *direct* legislative pressure has been applied, there was open and direct encouragement by the government, which felt Hebrew names would speed cultural and national homogeneity. Thus, for example, *Haaretz* reported that after the visit to South Africa of the Israeli ship *Misgav,* commanded by an officer with the non-Hebrew name of Vishnievsky, Ben Gurion informed the Chief of Staff that in the future "no officer will be sent abroad in a representative capacity unless he bears a Hebrew family name." He added that "soldiers, like civilians, are entitled to all the civil rights, including the doubtful 'right' [the quotation marks are in the original] to preserve their foreign family names." Following the example of government leaders, writers and columnists began to satirize Diaspora names. The result was the creation of a psychological climate that worked for the almost complete eradication of non-Hebrew family names. Despite those who feel that the traditional Jewish family names provide a colorful (albeit painful) illustration of Jewish history and that a name is too precious and too personal a matter to be tampered with, the Hebraizing process continues in Israel today.

The sources of the new Hebrew names are the Bible, the Talmud, and Midrashic literature. Those who cannot find names on their own come for help to the Commission on Names, which is part of the state Commission on Language. Most of the new names are short, of one or two syllables, and most are Hebrew, though some Aramaic forms have been used. Studies of thousands of family names have made it possible to classify a number of definite patterns which are in operation and by which names in Israel are being Hebraized. First of all, the foreign elements represented by German or Slavic suffixes -*wicz*, -*ev*, -*er*, -*ski*, -*chik*, -*mann*, -*son*, -*sohn*, -*baum*, -*berg*, -*stein*, etc., are removed. Generally, an effort is made to preserve some phonetic element of the old name, using one or more of the consonants and keeping one or more syllables: thus, Orbach becomes Or; Ornstein, Oren; Lubarsky, Bar; Goldenberg, Golan. (Golan is not only phonetically similar to Golden but it preserves the idea of *berg*, "mountain," "height"); Grozovsky, Gur; Goronchik, Goren; Dorfman, Doron; Osovsky, Asaf; Zokovsky, Zakai; Portnoy, Porat; Tzukerman and Tzchernowicz, Tzur; Tenenbaum, Tene; Polski, Pelles; Persky, Peres; Ruffer, Rafael; Nemirovsky, Namir; Narudetzki, Nardi; Wiedermann, Vardimon; Shreier, Sharir.

The same phonetic purpose is achieved in other cases by transposing consonants or syllables (metathesis): Ifland and Feldstein become Peled, as does Friedel ("p" and "f," and "b" and "v" are identical letters in Hebrew); Biber emerges as Rabib and Brodner gets transformed into Bendor and Kissner becomes Narkiss.

A name is changed by the substitution of Hebrew suffixes for Slavic and Germanic ones: Aronson and Aronowitch become Aroni; Yehielchik, Yehieli; Abramsohn, Abrami.

Foreign patronymics are frequently replaced with Semitic forms by using the Hebrew *ben*, the Arabic *ibn*, or the Aramaic *bar*: ben Tzvi, ibn Zahav, bar Yehuda, and Barnatan.

And we also have several matronymics in this form: ben Devorah and ben Rachel. These names then become real family names, and are passed down the generations and not limited to the original father-child relationship. But *ben* and *bar* are used in coined names also to indicate the relationship to an ideal or concept: ben Zohar ("son of light"); ben Horin ("son of freedom"); ben Shahar ("son of dawn"); ben Tikvah ("son of hope"); ben Zahav ("son of gold"); bar Gada ("son of good fortune").

The Hebrew prefixes *avi* ("father of") and *ahi* ("brother of") have come into widespread symbolic use. Symbolically they refer to the deity, as in Avigaal ("My God has saved"), Ahikam ("My God has risen"), Ahitov ("My God is good"). But in addition to this use, the prefix *avi* or *ahi* can actually refer to a specific individual: the archeologist Nachman Reiss changed his name to Avigad in honor of his son Gad; the playwright Mordecai Mandel changed his name to Avi-Shaul to honor his first-born, Shaul; and the poet Reuven Grossman changed his name to Avinoam in memory of his son, Noam, who was killed in the War of Independence.

Some names are translated: for example, Goldberg can become Harpaz ("mountain of gold"); Weintraub, Eshkol ("cluster of grapes") or Anav ("grape"); Idelson, Ben Yehuda or Bar Yehuda; Davidson, Ben David; Wolfsohn, Ben Zev.

The most widespread method of transforming a name has been by means of translating either in whole or part: Birnbaum becomes Agosi (*Birn* and *agos* mean "pear"); Teitelbaum, Tamari (*Teitel* and *tamar* mean "date"); Mandelstam, Sheked (*Mandel* and *sheked* mean "almond"); Nussbaum, Agozi (*Nuss* and *agoz* mean "nut"); Kirschenbaum, Duvdevani (*Kirsch* and *duvdevan* mean "cherry"); Rosenbaum, Vardi (*Rosen* and *vard* mean "rose"). Fisher and Riback similarly become Dayag ("fisher," in Hebrew); Kovalsky and Kuznitsky become Naphha ("smith," in Aramaic); Novick becomes Hadash ("new"); Wexler becomes Halfan ("money changer"); Jung becomes Elem ("young"); Recht becomes Amiti ("honest"); Lempert becomes Lavi ("leopard").

In the Bible, a number of names are found with theophoric prefixes or suffixes -*el*, -*eli*, -*ya*, -*yahu*. It appears that a number of people with deep religious convictions have selected this type of family name.

About 65 percent of the surnames received originally by German Jews are of geographic origin, and roughly the same proportion holds for East European Jews. In Israel, too, place names are common, but these have nothing to do with their bearers' origin. For example, the name Ophir does not mean that its bearer or his ancestors come from the place where Solomon got his gold; what has happened is that people once called Goldberg, Goldman, or Zolotovsky have taken the name of Ophir simply because of its association with the idea of gold. In the same way, Arnon does not refer to a person who once lived near the stream in ancient Moab but is taken because it bears a phonetic resemblance to Aronowitz, Aronowski, Ehrlich, Herling, just as Gilboa does to Gilbovsky, Gilberg, Golovsky.

There is a certain poetic justice in the attempts some Israelis have made to rectify the wrongs done more than a century and a half ago to their forefathers by Austrian and German officials: Inkdiger (*hinkediger*, "lame") has been changed to Adir ("strong"); Alter ("old") becomes Abrekh ("young"); Ungluck ("misfortune") has been transformed to Osher ("fortune"); and Lugner ("liar") to Amiti ("man of truth"). Traurig ("sad") now becomes Alyagon ("no sorrow"); Kabtzan ("destitute") becomes Nadiv ("noble," "rich"); and Schlechter ("bad") becomes Tuvi ("good").

Names expressing the emotions and sentiments of the new era that has begun with the State have also been popular choices. These names are built on roots like *dror* and *heruth* (both meaning "freedom"), *am* ("people"), and *tzur* ("rock"). Among the results are: Drori and Lidror ("my freedom"),

Heruti ("my freedom"), Amihai ("my people lives"), Amikam ("my people has risen"), Gildor ("generation of joy"), Amidror ("my free people"), Amiaz ("my people is strong"), Amitzur ("my people is a rock"), Amiram ("my people is high"), and Amiran ("my people sings").

Another kind of expressive name harks back to the disaster in Europe which preceded the birth of Israel: Nanod ("wanderer"), Sorid ("refugee"), Galmud ("lonely"), Kanai ("zealot"), Akshan ("determined"), Aldema ("no tears"), and Almagor ("no fear").

There are many new Israeli names that fit into no category. We must, therefore, assume that there was some very personal and private reason that determined its choice. If there were more information available, we could perhaps discover some clue to help us decipher the mystery. The following will illustrate this dramatically. I came across a Reichrudel who assumed the name Ben-Elul and a Kammerstein who changed his name to Tammuz. They do not fit any of the patterns described above. They both are names of a month on the Jewish calendar. Upon examining the family records, the mystery was resolved. Reichrudel was born on August 19, 1901, and Kammerstein's birthday is July 11. These dates correspond to the Hebrew months Elul and Tammuz respectively.

Not all changes of name in Israel are from non-Hebrew into Hebrew forms. But one gets the feeling that the process going on in Israel is an attempt to correct a wrong done to Jews in eastern and central Europe over a century ago. New Israeli family names may still not fit perfectly, but they have at least helped wipe out some painful associations. Artificial though it appears, the style of naming in Israel may serve as new skin to cover the blemishes and heal the scars of years gone by.

11

A Little Smarter than the Angels

A VISITOR ONCE COMMENTED to Niels Bohr, the Nobel Prize physicist: "I'm surprised to see that you have a horseshoe hanging over your door. Do you, a man dedicated to science, believe in that superstition?"

"Of course not," smiled Bohr, "but I've been told that it's supposed to be lucky whether you believe in it or not."

We all know people who still "knock wood" whenever they hear or utter a word of praise, without being aware that they are repeating an age-old magic ritual whose purpose is to distract or frighten away jealous spirits. Fear of the supernatural has produced a great number and variety of magic devices, and these protections have become our responses whenever we are afraid. In this sense magic was, and still is, an integral part of social usage; it has influenced not only folk habits but also religious ceremonials and rituals. Nor has modern, emancipated man completely broken the chain of past fears. We all are acquainted with persons who have given up their religion easily, but rarely their superstitions.

Side by side with the halakhic, authoritative legal system of Judaism, there developed a variety of practices, rituals, and beliefs that are usually grouped indiscriminately under the pejorative category of "superstitions." I prefer to call them folk religion, for in a real sense they spoke to the needs, the fears, and the perplexities that faced the ordinary folk, the unlearned men and women who could not always appreciate the dialectics and the definitions of the scholars and philosophers.

There are no "superstitions" or folk beliefs associated with Jewish family names, and the reason is obvious. It was the Age of Enlightenment that compelled Jews to adopt family names, and reason and superstition are incongruous. True, there were a number of individuals who, in selecting a family name, incorporated into it some reference, usually veiled, to a hopefully propitious future (such names are noted in the Dictionary). But for the most part Jewish family names, per se, are free of superstitions, although they do contain nonrational elements often if they are made up of first names. For Jewish first names, from the very beginning, were clothed in every kind of folk belief. In this chapter we will examine a number of these elements that were originally part of first names and which have come down to us both in the first names and as components of the family names.

Holle Kreisch

When the tradition of conferring a sacred name *(shem hakodesh)* and a secular name *(kinnui)* became widespread among Jews, a curious custom was adopted by the German Jews as early as the fourteenth century. On the fourth Sabbath after birth a ceremony called *Holle Kreisch* was observed. Children were invited to the new child's home, and they would form a circle around the cradle in which the infant lay. According to a set formula, the baby was lifted into the air three times and the guests shouted out: "Hollekreisch! What shall the child's name be?" And the appropriate response would be shouted: "Holle! Holle! The child's name will be . . ." By the seventeenth century this custom was observed in naming both boys and girls in South Germany, but it was performed for girls only in Austria, Bohemia, Moravia, and Poland. From there the ceremony spread to France, Holland, and the United States.

Rabbinic authorities were somewhat baffled by the ceremony and by the strange name, and some attempts were made to explain it as a combination of *hol* (from the Hebrew *hol*, "secular," "profane") and *kreischen* ("to call," "to shout out," in German), which would render it as "the ceremony of calling out the secular name." Scholars have determined, however, that this interpretation is artificial, contrived to explain the ceremony among Jews. Actually, this picturesque ceremony was borrowed directly from Gentile usage. In medieval Germany Holle was a demon-witch who carried off infants. When a child was born, the evil spirit had to be "called off," and that is what the ritual of Holle Kreisch is designed to do. The word is the name of the demon, Holle, plus a garbled version of the Hebrew word *kara* ("call"). Some derive *kreisch* from *kreisen* ("to encircle"), and say the ceremony means encircling Holle to protect the child. Since circumcision was deemed a sufficient safeguard for boys, the Holle Kreisch was at first performed by Jews in the case of girls only.

To Name or Not to Name After the Living

It was a widespread belief among all ancient peoples that "a man's name is the essence of his being"; it was considered a part of him in the same way as is a vital part of his body or a trait of his character. Because of this mystical identity, people believed that to give the name of one living person to another would transfer his being, his individuality, to the other person, with the result that the one from whom the name is taken must cease to exist.

And the same consideration would prevent people from naming after deceased relatives or ancestors. To give the child the name of a departed ancestor—according to the Biblical evidence—would destroy and obliterate the soul and the remembrance of the departed and cause his soul to forsake its peaceful abode in heaven. This may explain why names are not repeated in the Biblical period. It was impossible for two persons belonging to the same family or group to have the same name.

In the Talmudic period the growing practice of naming children after ancestors indicates that there developed a modification of the belief in the absolute identity of the name with the person. More and more did the belief develop that by giving a child the name of an ancestor the memory of the deceased would thereby be preserved and kept alive. To pass on one's name to one's offspring is, in fact, to be "born anew" and thus to perpetuate one's being. To this belief was added the notion that the "personality" of a new-born infant can be protected from demonic assault by being "screened" or "covered" by that of an older or distinguished individual. This is accomplished by conferring upon it the same name.

This was true not only in the case of deceased relatives; it was also true in the case of individuals who were alive. Not only were people not afraid of their lives when others were named for them, but they were even pleased with it and welcomed it, since it meant that the preservation of their memory was thus assured them. Thus, Rabbi Nathan had children named after him by grateful parents (Shabbat 134A and Hullin 47B) and Rabbi Eliezer ben Shimon was honored the same way (Baba Metzia 84B). Throughout the Talmudic period we find people naming their children not only after departed ancestors; there was also no hesitancy to name children after living parents, grandparents, relatives, or friends.

In the post-Talmudic period two diverse naming practices are followed by the Ashkenazim and Sephardim. Among the Sephardim there is no fear of hesitancy in naming a child after a living person. There are many instances of a grandson being given the name of his grandfather when the latter was still alive. The most illustrious Hebrew poet of the Spanish golden age, Judah Halevi, mentions in one of his poems his grandson Judah. And there is also Rabbi Isaiah de Trani, a leading Italian rabbinical authority of the thirteenth century, who was named after his living grandfather, Isaiah de Trani the Elder. And when the daughter-in-law of Nahmanides (Moses ben Nachman, the *Ramban*), who was the daughter of Rabbi Jonah Girondi, gave birth to a son, Nahmanides, the paternal grandfather of the baby, in a spirit of magnanimity, declared: "Although, as custom requires, the child should be called by my name (Moses), I will forego the privilege and am willing that he be called Jonah, in honor of his maternal grandfather."

We also find among the Sephardim the practice of calling a son by the name of his father when his father is still living. This practice, however, is less frequent and is not accepted by all Sephardim. But Jacob Saphir mentions in his travelogue *Even Saphir* that among the Jews of Yemen it is a custom to give a child the name of his father, especially in a family that had previously lost children. Among some Sephardim of Jerusalem, it was believed that a father would be assured a long life if he named his son after himself. It would appear that among the Sephardim there was a strong belief that whatever mistakes the Angel of Death might make by confusing the names of two living relatives bearing the identical name, it would be in favor of the person whose life he was seeking to terminate.

Ashkenazim, however, preferred to play it safe and did not want to rely on the hope that the Angel of Death would make a mistake in favor of the living. The reverse might happen. Hence, with but very few exceptions, the general practice among the Ashkenazim has been *not* to name a child after a living parent or relative. That this practice is based only on superstition is frankly admitted by the authorities, but they believe in safety first. Thus, in the *Sefer Hasidim* we find: "Superstitions work harm only upon those who are concerned about them. Non-Jews call their sons by the names of their fathers and no harm results. But the Jews are careful not to do so." In another instance, Rabbi Judah Hahasid, the author of *Sefer Hasidim,* states, almost apologetically: "Although one should not believe in superstitions, it is better to be careful."

It would seem that the hesitancy on the part of the Ashkenazim to name children after living parents and grandparents was engendered by the ancient idea of the absolute identity of the soul, the very being of a person, with his name. This older idea, so prominent in the Biblical era, was revived and found strong expression among the German mystics, some of whom went even further and objected that their descendants will be named after them when they die. Thus, Rabbi Judah Hahasid declared in his will that none of his descendants shall be called Judah, or by his father's name, Samuel. However, his insistence is an exception to the rule that prevailed almost universally of preferring to have descendants named after departed ancestors.

"Trans-sexual" Names

Since having a descendant assume one's name was symbolic of being reborn again and some people considered it a misfortune to be reborn a woman, there were some authorities who objected to giving a girl the name of a male ancestor, and vice versa. In spite of these objections the practice has become widespread and is responsible for certain names being especially popular among Jews. Mindel became a very common name for a girl as the equivalent of Mendel, and Mashe is very often given to a girl named for a Moshe. We have already noted that in the State of Israel so many of the Biblical names for males have become "suitable" for girls by adding a feminine suffix. Actually already in the Bible a number of names are common to both men and women; Abijah (mother of Hezekiah and a son of Samuel and a king of Judah); Ataliah (a leading Benjamite and the daughter of Ahab and Jezebel); Ephah (Caleb's concubine and a male descendant of Judah); Shelomit (daughter of Zerubavel and the name of a man); Gomer (son of Japhet and wife of Hosea); and Noadjah (a Levite and a prophetess). In the Talmud, too, Pazzi and Yohanan were used by both men and women. Shalom was a woman's name; today it is a common male name.

In the Middle Ages we find Yeruham, Mazal-Tov, Nehamah, Menuhah, Simhah, and Tamar being used at times for men, at other times for women. Such common names may not be very numerous but they are recorded. This is true not only of the Jewish tradition but of English names as well. In the eighteenth century Lucy, Ann, and Caroline were recorded as boys' names. And today a number of names are used both by boys and girls: Leslie, Sydney, Terry, Lee, Alva, Meredith, and Adrian, for example.

In spite of the apprehensions expressed by some medieval authorities, it became a common practice to name a grandson after his grandmother (or other female relatives) and a granddaughter after her grandfather (or other male relatives).

Change of Name as a Remedy

Since, as we have seen, names were considered of special importance and deemed synonymous with an individual's personality, it followed that when a change took place in the person, there must be a corresponding change in the person's name. New names were frequently adopted when it was desired to invest a person with a new identity. Thus, we find in the Bible Abram's name changed to Abraham and Sarai's name changed to Sarah as a sign that they were to play a new role in the history of mankind. Jacob becomes Israel after the decisive struggle at the ford of Jabbok. Hoshea becomes Joshua when he is called to a special destiny and Gideon is given a new name, Yerubaal, after destroying the altar of the idol Baal. Sometimes the kings of Judah received new names upon ascending the throne (a practice that has been followed by kings and popes to this day)—thus Eliakim becomes King Yehoiakim and Mattaniah becomes King Zedekiah (2 Kings 23:34; 24:17).

Similarly, because a change of name conferred a new personality a convert to Judaism is given a new name—X the son of Abraham, our Patriarch, and Y the daughter of Abraham, our Patriarch.

The Talmud (Rosh Hashanah 16B) states that four things abrogate the evil decree—charity, prayer, a change in behavior, and the change of one's name. During the Middle Ages this last suggestion became an important weapon in anti-demonic strategy. Outsmarting the evil spirits figures prominently in the rituals of many peoples, but medieval Jews resorted to this device only rarely. It was most commonly employed in changing the name of a gravely ill person so that the Angel of Death would be unable to find him.

Jews visualized the celestial administration as conducted in much the same bureaucratic fashion as a mundane government. God distributes His decrees among various departments or agencies, and the tasks are assigned to various angels and spirits for execution. The angels follow their orders to the letter, never deviating; they go only by names and addresses. And if they come to the given address and, looking there for a person with a certain name, do not find such a person, they

report back that they could not find him. The matter is
dropped and the verdict is destroyed. There was, therefore,
always the possibility of outwitting the heavenly cohorts.
Moses of Coucy, the thirteenth-century French rabbi, elabo-
rates the Talmudic dictum on changing one's name and
explains that the person who changes his name as much as tells
the angel looking for him: "I am not the person you are
seeking. I am not the one who committed the sins you charge
me with." And, of course, the angel takes him at his word. In
the Middle Ages, the belief was prevalent—especially among
German Jews—that changing the name of a sick person could
save his life. This practice has continued to this day and there
are still many Jews who, when everything else has failed, turn
to this as a last resort.

The changing of one's name developed into a solemn
ritual, conducted in the presence of a *minyan* (a quorum of
ten men) by a reader who holds the Torah scroll and repeats a
formula ascribed to the days of the great Babylonian academies. During the Middle Ages the customary procedure was to
find a new name "by lot": a Bible would be opened at random
and the first name that appeared was chosen. Today, when a
name is changed, the name selected is usually one which in
itself suggests a long life or a prayer that God will heal or
strengthen the patient: Hayyim ("life"); Alter ("old," i.e., may
he grow to be an old man). Some derive Alter from the Latin
alter ("another"). The person says to the Angel of Death: "I
am not the one you want; I am Alter, someone else." The
feminine equivalent is Alte. Zayde ("grandfather," i.e., may he
grow to be a grandfather); Bobe ("grandmother"); Shalom
("peace," i.e., may peace and safety be assured him); Raphael
("God heals"); Azriel ("God helps"); Hezekiah and Ezekiel
("God strengthens")—are names taken in dangerous situations
also because of their meaning.

After announcing the new name, the heavenly authorities
are formally notified of the change and requested to consider

the person as not identical with the one who bore his former name, "for he is another man, like a new-born infant, who has just been born unto a long and good life." The new name then becomes the true name and is used in all religious documents.

However, since Jews were traditionally known by their parent's names as well as by their own (Isaac son of Abraham, Dinah daughter of Jacob) the patient's life was still not completely protected. There was still the chance that the Angel of Death may be looking for him as the child of his parents; the death warrant might just state "child of X and Y." To meet this danger, a very ingenious practice was developed—changing his parents' names, too! This was done not by giving the parents another name but by giving the child other parents, as it were. The real parents would "sell" their sick child to another couple who, because their children were alive and well, appeared to be in high favor with the heavenly powers. Thus, the child acquired a new name *and* new parents, and the Angel of Death was pretty confused by this time. And if his orders were to punish the parents by taking their child away from them, he finds that these parents no longer have a child.

There are a number of variations in the practice of "selling" a child to other parents. A parent would sometimes publicly "renounce" his relationship to the child, and a relative would adopt the child as his own. In some communities of North Africa a child who was dangerously ill would be sold not to an individual but to the *hevra kaddisha*, the official organization of the Jewish community. In a number of communities the child would be "sold" and given the name Tzion or Ben Tzion, child of Zion, i.e., belonging to the entire community of Israel.

The following is an excerpt from a formula of redemption for a child on the island of Rhodes who was given the name Mercado: "Up to now you are under the authority of your father and mother; henceforth, you will be under the authority of your Father in Heaven and under the authority of Rabbi Meir the miracle worker who will protect you from all evil." At the beginning of every month, the child's mother would kindle an oil lamp, cast a coin into the oil, and send the coin to the shrine of Rabbi Meir in Tiberias, Israel.

Scholars have traced a number of names that are really terms associated with the marketplace—terms such as selling, purchasing, redeeming, bartering, exchanging—to the practice of "selling" a child to new parents. Thus, a name like Mercado ("market") and Comprado ("bought") are not real names but a symbol that the child has been "bought" by a new set of parents and is thereby "redeemed" from death. Some scholars trace the practice back to the Talmudic period and identify such names as Tahlifa and Halafta (from the root that means "exchange") as such symbolic names. Among the Jews of France in the Middle Ages there often occurs the name Matzif which is really a garbled version of Emancipé ("liberated," "freed," i.e., from the power of death). The name Meshulam ("paid for," i.e., "bought") also hints at this tradition of selling a sick child to new parents.

Apotropaic Names

A number of names are in the category of apotropaisms, a means of warding off danger and evil. Either the name itself serves as a *segulah*, a curative power, or it is part of a ritual, the purpose of which is to neutralize the power of the Angel of Death. Almost all of these names have to do with a child whose parents' previously born children have died. If we consider the staggering general rate of infant mortality during the Middle Ages and the specially insalubrious condition of the cramped Jewish ghettos, it comes as no surprise that, in addition to all kinds of amulets and magic used to frustrate the wiles of Lilith and her band of demons, a complete assortment of protective and therapeutic names would also be employed.

The most effective treatment was to give the child, who was struggling to survive or whose siblings had died before his birth, a name that signifies life, and the name most commonly selected was Hayyim, which means "life." The antiquity of its use is attested by the fact that it appears on the Jewish catacombs of Venosa, Italy, in its Latin form, Vita. Some have derived Hayyim from the Spanish Jaime (Jacob) because of the similarity of pronunciation, but Hayyim was probably long established among Jews before the Spanish name took on its modern sound.

Hayyim appears as Aim in Spain, as Haguin, Haquin, Hagin, in France. In Germany it became Hain and Hein and Heinemann (whence the family name of Heinrich Heine). It was translated as Vives, Feivish, Vivant, Vis, Fis, Vivelman, Feivelman, Feibelman among the Jews of France and Germany in the Middle Ages. Among Italian Jews it took the form of Vivanti, Vidal, and Vital, which became Feitel among the Jews in Germany. In Byzantium the translation of Hayyim was Polychronos ("much time," "life") and Polyzotos ("may he live long").

For a girl the common Hebrew forms were Hayyah and Havah. Jewish women in Greece took the name Zoë ("life") and in Spain the girls were called Vida.

The Hebrew Hai was also used as a *segulah* when previous children did not survive, and the meaning was "may he live," "may he survive." In France both Hai and Hayyim were used; in Italy Hai was preferred; and in Germany Hayyim was used nearly exclusively.

Hayyim has three interesting forms of a *kinnui:* Leblang, Meisterlin, and Lutz. Leblang means "live long"; Meisterlin means "a little master" and expresses the prayer that he grow to be a little man; and Lutz, though understood by some scholars as a diminutive for Ludwig, actually is a Germanized version of the Hebrew *luz*. There are two interesting rabbinic traditions associated with *luz*. One states that *luz* is the name of a bone in the spinal column that is indestructible. In the days of the Messiah, when the resurrection of the dead will take place, this bone will be the source of new life for every human being. A second tradition identifies *luz* as the name of a city over which the Angel of Death has no power. Both references associate *luz* with life and survival, and Lutz, therefore became an appropriate *kinnui* for Hayyim.

In the interest of comparative folklore, it may be noted that among the peasants of Bulgaria it is a custom to name a child born after the death of a first child Zhivko ("life") if a boy and Zhivka if a girl, to insure the child's life.

Another name used in the apotropaic ritual of changing names, Gronim or Gronimann, derived from Geronymos (from the Greek *geron,* "old man"), was given to a child because of its dual therapeutic qualities. First of all it expressed the hope that this child would live to attain the age of an old man. Secondly, it could be used in a ruse. If the Angel of Death came to claim the child, he could declare, "You have the wrong person. There is no child here, only an old man."

The Latin *matrona,* in the form Madrona, was used as an apotropaic name even before Alte (feminine of Alter, "old one") came into use. Mata and Matla, names commonly found in the German Jewish ghettos before the modern period, are derivatives of *matrona.* Their purpose is to express the hope that the little girl would live to become a mother. The names Gnanna and Gnendel are also in this category and are the equivalent of Bobe ("grandmother," in Yiddish), for Gnanna is grandmother in old German.

When an infant was orphaned of both his parents, he was given the *kinnui* of Vives ("life") and his *shem hakodesh* was Uri Shraga (both words mean "light") as a symbolic reference to the two departed souls. Some scholars define the name Shneur (which means "two lights") as having originated in such a tragic circumstance also.

In Hosea 14:4 there is the phrase "for in Thee, the orphan finds mercy *(yeruham)*." As a result, an orphan would often be given the religious name of Yeruham and the *kinnui* Fishel (as a form of Vivs, "life"). Yeruham has also been used as a name for girls. Often the names that express consolation for the loss of a parent or of an older brother or sister are used for both sexes. Thus, Simhah ("joy"), originally a name for women (as it still is among the Sephardim) is a common boy's name among the Ashkenazim; Nehamah ("consolation"), a girl's name, is also used for boys.

The following names all express blessing and consolation and were conferred upon a new-born child following the death of his older sibling: Eliakim ("may God preserve"); to this was often added as *kinnui* the name Anastos (from the Greek Anastasios, "resurrected"); Paragoros (from the Greek "soothing," as a translation of the Hebrew name Menahem, "comforter"). Paragoros is one of the oldest names among Jews; it is mentioned in the Palestinian Talmud and is found in the inscriptions on the sarcophagi of Beth Shearim. It is also found on the list of martyrs during the massacres in the Rhineland in 1096. Durante ("lasting," "enduring") is another name of comfort; Troestlin ("consolation") is a *kinnui* for Nehemiah among German Jews and appears both as a masculine and feminine name in the garbled version of Trestel. Among Italian Jews we find the name Consolo as a family name and Consolina as a woman's name.

Another method of safeguarding the life of a child is to give it an *ugly* name. This protective measure is also found among the Chinese. They give the infant his first name (called a milk name) at the age of one month. This name is usually a contemptible appellation. It is hoped that the evil spirits will thus not consider the child worth their attention. A remarkable parallel is found in Jewish tradition, and one of the oldest references to it is found in the Midrash. In a comment on Numbers 12:1 where the Bible states that Moses had married a Cushite, an Ethiopian, the Midrash states: "Because of her beauty she was called a Cushite, just as a man calls his handsome son a Cushite so that the Evil Eye will have no power over him."

This kind of protective measure could explain the origin of such Germanic names as Schwartzmann ("black man"), Moreno (Spanish for "dark"), and the female name Charna (Slavic for "black"). Moreno is often confused with Morenu ("our teacher," in Hebrew), which has another origin and meaning.

Despite the long-standing tradition among Jews not to give a child a name that occurs in the Bible before the time of Abraham, Havah (Eve) was acceptable in the Middle Ages and after because "She was the mother of all living" (Genesis 3:20). Noah, too, had the distinction of being righteous and faultless (Genesis 6:9) and therefore was considered a fitting name even though it was pre-Abrahamitic. Noah often served as a substitute for the comforting Menahem, since both derive from the same Hebrew root meaning "to comfort," and thus had the added feature of being an expression of solace and consolation.

Enoch has the unique distinction of having "walked with God" (Genesis 5:24). But Enoch became an acceptable name not because of his reputation on earth but because he was transported to heaven ("for God took him"). In the vernacular Enoch became Henach, and to it was attached the *kinnui* Zundel, a corruption of Söhnlein ("little son"). Zundel-Henach remains a popular name combination to this day. There is also an old German form Näarlein, which appears as early as 1298, that is a curious hybrid of the Hebrew *naar* ("lad") plus the German diminutive suffix *-lin*. A clue to the connection between Enoch and a little child is offered in the literature of the mystics, where we find the angel Metatron (the name means "the one behind the Heavenly Throne") identified with Enoch. In the pseudepigraphic *Book of Enoch* we are informed that Metatron dwells in heaven and gathers together the souls of all still-born children and of all infants and school children who have died and brings them beneath the Heavenly Throne. He conducts classes for the little ones in the study of Torah.

What a comfort it must have been for parents, when they conferred the name Hanoch (Enoch) -Zundel or Hanoch-Näarlein upon an infant whose older brother had died. There was, first of all, the symbolic reminder in the name that the heavenly Enoch was looking after the departed little one; and there was also the security for the new child, since he identified with the archangel, against whom neither Satan nor the Angel of Death has any power.

Names of Angels

Names of angels were rarely used by Jews during the first half of the Middle Ages; they were, however, very common among Christians. The name Michael was especially popular in the Byzantine Empire, and it appears that it is here that Jews first adopted the custom of using the names of angels. From Byzantium the practice spread to the Jews of Italy and thence to Jewish communities in other parts of Europe. Oriental Jews picked up the custom even later. In fact, the first one among them bearing such a name is Rabbi Gabriel ben Eliyahu who lived in the sixteenth century. From this time onward the names of angels become more and more common among Oriental Jews both in the Holy Land and elsewhere.

Raphael, Michael, and Gabriel were usually selected for the purpose of protecting the new-born infants. Uriel does not appear and in its place we find, among the Jews of Persia and Mesopotamia, the name Nuriel. The most popular apotropaic name of this group is Raphael ("God shall heal") which is also the name most frequently inscribed in amulets worn by expectant mothers. In time, Raphael became the name most often conferred upon a sick child and the most popular name which was given to a person in the ritual of changing the name.

Names of Animals

Among Ashkenazic Jews the custom of giving children names of animals (Baer, Wolff, Loeb, Herz) became especially widespread when the use of a separate religious name and secular designation was introduced. Here was an imaginative combination which seemed almost to enjoy the sanction of the Bible itself, since it was derived from the blessings of the patriarch Jacob conferred upon his sons (Genesis 49), in which he compares some of their qualities to animals.

An additional incentive to using these names was provided by some of the popular beliefs current among Jews and their neighbors. It was generally believed that the strength and energy of an animal could, in some magical way, be transferred to an infant as a source of vitality and power. These beliefs were further substantiated by the fact that the word for wild animal in Hebrew (and also in Yiddish), *hayah*, also means "a living thing." Special preference, of course, was given to the wild animals which are mentioned by Jacob in his blessing (Genesis 49).

While we have some evidence of Italian Jews using animal names in a very limited degree during the Middle Ages, this style of naming is completely unknown to the Jews of North Africa and Yemen, and to Sephardim generally. To this day, in Israel, many Sephardim continue to be amazed and amused by the menagerie that are found in the households of their Ashkenazi neighbors.

Names Determine Destiny

A name, it was believed, not only determines a person's character, but also his fate. Certain names bring good fortune, others bad. In the Talmud we already find an admonition against naming a child after a wicked person. The rabbis point to the grim example of Doeg, whose mother daily donated to the Temple the increase of his weight in gold. During the siege of Jerusalem she slaughtered and ate the child. And all this because she chose the name of a wicked man for him (Yoma 38B). The Midrash advises: "One should examine names carefully in order to give his son a name that is worthy, so that the son may become a righteous person, for sometimes the name is a contributing factor for good as for evil."

It was, therefore, considered the height of imprudence to confer upon a child the name of a person who met with a violent death, lest the sad fate of the former bearer of that name also befall the one named after him. The same fear is behind the hesitation to name a child after a person who died young or childless. Sometimes the name of the person who died young is combined with the name of another person who was blessed with longevity and the two names are conferred. In the same way the name of one who died childless is combined with the name of another person who was blessed with many children. Thus, the name of the departed is preserved and, at the same time, the fear of the superstition is avoided.

The same fear prevents some parents from naming their child after another child of theirs who died. Most rabbinic authorities, however, declare it permissible. Some authorities, however, advise, for safety's sake, to combine the dead child's name with another name, and call the new child by the two names.

Some authorities would even permit two living children in

the same family to be called by one and the same name. They cite the case of Rabbi Hisda who had two sons who bore the same name. It is, however, thought advisable to avoid such practice for fear of the "Evil Eye."

Some religious authorities have even maintained that a widow or widower should not marry a person with the same name as the deceased mate, but this is rarely followed.

It was a widespread folk belief among Jews during the Middle Ages that, confronted with two individuals of the same name, the ministering angels were as likely as not to choose the wrong one. Therefore, some maintained that several families with a common name should not reside in one dwelling. People went so far as to avoid entering the home of a sick person who bore their name, lest the Angel of Death arrive during the visit and take the wrong soul.

This same kind of superstition brought about the admonition against a marriage if the bride has the same name as the groom's mother or the bride's father has the same name as the groom, to prevent mistaking two persons by the same name in one family if a punishment is to be inflicted by Heaven. The danger is especially great where respective parents of a married couple have the same name and patrynomic. In such cases the angel will be absolutely at a loss to distinguish the one from the other.

Only Hebrew Is Spoken in Heaven

While a few authorities object to using non-Hebrew or non-Jewish names, the majority recognize that even in Talmudic times the practice was widespread. The use of the religious name is preferred, however, when a person is called up to the Torah and in certain prayers recited in behalf of the person.

The need for calling a person by a Hebrew name in connection with the recitation of prayers is based upon the belief that the official language of the heavenly administration and celestial court is Hebrew, and that the angels are monolingual. The ministering angels were not believed to be great linguists and would, therefore, ignore or fail to understand any communication addressed in a language other than Hebrew. In Heaven, a Jew can be recognized only by his Hebrew name.

It was also believed that as soon as a person dies and is buried, the Angel of Death comes to his grave and asks him for his name for the purpose of examining his earthly record. Unless the deceased can give his name in Hebrew, his case cannot be processed, and his entry into Heaven will be delayed. It is, therefore, necessary for every Jew to remember his Hebrew name. To facilitate this, a memory aid is included in the traditional prayerbook, so that by the daily recitation of a verse from the Bible, which contains his/her name, the person will be sure to remember it.

But as important as it is to know one's Hebrew name at the beginning of one's sojourn to Heaven, it is even more crucial to know the name at the time of the Resurrection. For when the Messiah comes and the dead are revived, every resident in Heaven must respond to the final roll call with his Hebrew name.

Another peculiar practice in regard to accurate identification in dealing with the heavenly authorities is the custom of adding to one's name the name of one's mother and not that of one's father. Thus, while in the Memorial Service the name of the departed and his/her father's name is used, in the special prayer recited in behalf of the sick, the name of the patient's mother is included. This is the only case where the traditional patronymic is not used. This practice is associated in the Talmud with the reference in Psalms 116:16, where David pleads, "I am Thy servant, child of Thy handmaid."

The tradition was reinstituted by the kabbalists under the influence of the Zohar and has become widespread among Jews.

Who Selects a Name?

There are no fixed regulations of inflexible rules in the matter of who selects a child's name. In the Bible, usually the father chose the name, but in many instances the mother did so. Sometimes a foster mother, as in the case of Moses, or neighbors, as in the case of the child of Ruth and Boaz (Ruth 4:17) choose a name. In one case the father named his son (Solomon) and the prophet gave him an additional name (Yedidiah). There is no information in the Talmud on this, and it can be assumed that the Biblical traditions were continued. In the Midrashic literature we find several references to names given by both parents. In some communities today there is a popular custom for the mother to select the name of her first-born and to name it after *her* parents or relatives. Some religious authorities, however, insist that it is the father's prerogative. In actual practice, these questions are usually settled between the parents.

When Is the Child Named?

In the Biblical era a child was given a name at its birth. In Talmudic times, although no specific regulation can be found, the usual custom was to name the male child at his circumcision, and this has become the established practice ever since. If the circumcision is postponed because of illness, the naming is also postponed. In the special cases (such as the child who is a hemophiliac) when the child remains uncircumcized, the name is given when the father is called up to the Torah in the synagogue. There is a difference of rabbinic opinion as to whether it is preferable to do so before the child is eight days old or after.

In the case of girls there has been no uniform practice. Among the Sephardim in the Middle East the naming of a girl is a home ceremony. The parents invite guests, at which time the daughter's name is announced. Italian Jews customarily name girls in the synagogue on the first Sabbath when the mother is able to be there after childbirth. Ashkenazim name girls in the synagogue on the Sabbath or on a Monday or Thursday when the father is called to the Torah.

The special prayer recited at the naming of a boy has been incorporated into the circumcision ritual. Among the Sephardim, the formula recited in naming a girl is: "May He who blessed Sarah, Rebecca, Rachel and Leah, Miriam the prophetess, Abigail and Queen Esther daughter of Avihayil, bless this baby girl, and may her name be called 'X' daughter of 'Y,' with a good omen *(mazal tov)* and in a blessed hour."

The Ashkenazic prayer for naming a girl is: "May He who blessed our fathers Abraham, Isaac, and Jacob bless also the mother 'X' the daughter of 'Y' and her daughter born with a good omen. May her name in Israel be 'A' the daughter of 'B' and may her parents be privileged to rear her to the marriage canopy and to a life of good deeds, Amen."

PART II

A DICTIONARY
OF SELECTED
JEWISH NAMES

1

Determining the Origins of Your Family and Its Name

THE MEANING OF your particular family name depends upon a number of factors. The place of residence of the ancestor who assumed it makes a great deal of difference in the derivation of its meaning. Suppose the name is Lefkowitz (Lewkowitz). If your forebears came from Poland or Russia, the name is a patronymic, derived from Lev or Levke, which means "lion," and is a translation of Layb or Laybel ("lion,"in Yiddish), the *kinnui* of Judah. The Slavic suffix *-wich* or *-wicz* indicates "son of," and the name means "son of Yehuda [Judah] Laybel." But if your forebears are Hungarian Jews, then the name Lefkowitz is derived from the town Lewocza (Locse), formerly in Hungary but now in Slovakia, and the name therefore is geographic in origin.

Or suppose your family name is Balaban. Then you have a number of possible derivations. In certain parts of Russia, the name Balaban means "falcon" and the name may indicate one who lived in or near a house with the sign of a falcon, and it would be a house-sign name. But your ancestor may also have been in some occupation or trade associated with falcons, so that the same name would be occupational. In the Ukraine, Balaban means "apple fritter" and perhaps your ancestor owned a wayside inn famous for this delicacy. In Bulgaria, and in some other Balkan districts, Balaban means "great." Professor Meir Balaban, the famous Jewish historian of Poland, derived his name from this last definition, and took it as the translation of the Hebrew Gedaliah. The name can thus be a patronymic and as such ("great man") is the Balkan equivalent of the German Grossman ("great man"). Thus we see that the same name may have different derivations depending on the origin and circumstances of the family.

A family name derived from a place is not always an indication that, at the time when the name was assumed, the family actually lived in that place. Sometimes, such names reflect the vicissitudes and changing fortunes of the Jews in other ways. Thus, for example, the Chmielnicki pogroms of 1648–1649 caused many Polish Jews to flee to Silesia and Moravia, and among the communities of refuge was Leipnik, Moravia. Later, some returned to Poland and recalled the community that had given them refuge by assuming the name Leitner.

In 1746 Frederick the Great expelled the Jews from Silesia, and most of the Jews of Breslau had to leave. When, later, these had to assume a family name, they remembered nostalgically their place of origin in the names Breslau, Breslauer, and Bressler, though at the time they no longer lived in the Silesian city.

When Prussia took over sections of Poland and Lithuania, in 1772, many Jews were expelled to areas of Poland under Russian domination. In 1804, when Czar Alexander I ordered the Jews to assume permanent family names, many took the names of the places of their family's origin more than three decades earlier.

Many who bear the name Cohen or Levin are surprised to discover that they are not of priestly or Levitic lineage. The reason for this is that the name Cohen or Levin could have been the mother's maiden name. A number of Jews adopted the mother's name because of various exigencies, the most vexing of which was the repressive measure of the *Familianten Gesetz*. This was the law that was promulgated in 1726 in Bohemia, Moravia, and Silesia, and required every Jew to obtain a special permit before he could marry. Its purpose was severely to restrict the number of Jewish marriages. Only one son in a family could marry, and the number of permits issued was limited to the number of deaths in the Jewish community. Jews, however, often evaded this law by marrying secretly according to the Jewish ritual only and not registering the marriage in the groom's family name but in his mother's name. Others used the mother's name to avoid conscription into the army, especially in Russia, while others may have picked up a forged document in order to flee the country.

I know of one family whose name was Kotlar in Poland and changed it to Levin in America, because Levin seemed more "American" to them. The second generation Americanized it even further into the Irish Lennon.

In the final analysis, the only certain way of verifying one's family name is by means of some kind of family record. Without such a record, there is always the possibility of a mistaken derivation.

Many of us harbor a secret desire to be the scions of illustrious families. Especially if our names are Frankel, Horowitz, Halperin, Landau, Bachrach, Ginsburg, Epstein, or Altschul, who are so numerous. Still, we would like to feel that we are descendants of those who *originated* the family name rather than the masses who merely *imitated* and *copied* the name. Here, again, only a careful family record can determine the true facts. Without such a record we have no way of proving our illustrious lineage. I suppose, however, we could be like the Midwesterner who was traveling through a small New England town and stopped at an antique shop where he spotted a pair of early American portraits; he questioned the proprietor about them.

"Them's ancestors," the owner said.

"Ancestors? *Whose* ancestors?" the visitor pursued.

"Anyone's a mind to claim 'em," the enterprising Yankee replied with a wink.

The following Dictionary of names—some more distinguished, some less—are "anyone's a mind to claim 'em!"

2

Introduction to Dictionary

It would be an impossible task to attempt to include all Jewish names. Before the Holocaust it was estimated that there were about seventy-five thousand different kinds of Jewish family names all over the world, encompassing every language that Jews have ever used. With the destruction of Jewish life in most of Europe a number of these names probably disappeared, but new events have set in motion a variety of new naming processes that have created many new name forms, both personal and family.

I have selected for the dictionary only a sampling of names to illustrate what has been taking place among Jews for the past four millennia.

About Pronunciation and Transliteration

The Hebrew poet Hayyim Nahman Bialik once said that one cannot really translate from one language into another. It is, as Bialik put it, "like kissing one's sweetheart through a veil." If this is true of translations, then transliterations pose even greater problems and the results are even less satisfying.

Take, for example, the Germanic name Baum. Among German-speaking Jews it is pronounced like the German word for "tree," *Baum*. But Polish, Hungarian, and Russian Jews pronounce the same name Boym (in western Yiddish); Lithuanian Jews pronounce it as Beym (rhyming with "tame"), in what is scientifically called eastern Yiddish. Sometimes these variations will be indicated in the Index.

Although I have used a popular Sephardic Hebrew transliteration, because that has become standard, especially since the establishment of the Jewish state, where it is the dialect spoken, it often misrepresents the sounds familiar to those Ashkenazic ancestors who bore many of the names in this book. Therefore, occasionally I have departed from the Sephardic in order to be more accurate about those of our forefathers who lived in Poland, Lithuania, Galicia, Russia, etc.

Symbols for Identification

The reader has become familiar with a variety of methods that have been used since the end of the eighteenth century to create the many different names we find among Jews today. I have attempted to organize these name forms into eleven categories and have assigned a symbol of identification for each category:

- (A)   Acronyms and abbreviations.
- (C)   Names that indicate "son-in-law of."
- (D)   Names which refer to descriptive features, appearance, some personal characteristic.
- (F)   Fanciful names. Names that were imaginatively invented.
- (G)   Geographical, place names.

(H) Names derived from medieval and early modern house signs.

(L) Lineage, indicating family of priests or Levites.

(M) Matronymic names derived from the mother or other female ancestor.

(O) Names derived from one's occupation, trade, or profession.

(P) Patronymic names derived from one's father or paternal ancestor.

(S) A name derived from one's wife, indicating "husband of." In the broader sense this category is also a matronymic. In Jewish tradition this kind of name held a special place, because the woman of the house often became the breadwinner so that the man could pursue sacred studies.

In the case where a name is a combination of two or more categories, more than one symbol is noted in the following Dictionary. The symbols are joined together by the conjunction *and*. In the case of a name that may have more than one meaning, the symbols are linked by the conjunction *or* to indicate the alternatives. The first symbol listed is generally accepted as the most common, the second symbol, the less frequent, etc.

3

A Dictionary
of Selected Jewish Names

Many names discussed in Part I are not listed here. The reader can find their derivations by locating the text discussion in the Index of Names, as well as further discussion in Part I, or within the Dictionary, of names that do not have separate entries here.

Note: *Kinnui* is a noun that first appears in the Talmud. It means "surname," "by-name," or "substitute name." It derives from the Biblical verb meaning "to give an epithet." In the Middle Ages, Jews made a distinction between a Hebrew or sacred first name *(shem hakodesh)* and a secular name that related to it in some way. The secular first name is called the *kinnui.*

AARON (P) The following are common derivatives of this name: Agron, Agronsky, Aren, Arkin, Arkush, Orlik, Orun.

ABBA (P) *or* (A) An Aramaic personal name from the Talmudic period. Some families adopted this name as an acronym for *Avo Begevurot Adonai* (Psalm 71:16), "may I come into thy strength, Lord" ("strength" is symbolically associated with the age of eighty).

ABEL (P) Sometimes a diminutive of Abba, but most often a

diminutive of Abraham (Avraham). Avraham becomes Avril, Avil, Abil, Abel. Sometimes this last form appears as Apel or Appel, since the letters "b" and "p" are interchangeable.

ABRABANEL, ABRAVANEL (P) A diminutive of Abravan, a form for Abraham among Spanish Jews. The name has often been transposed to Abarbanel. Its use among non-Sephardic families attests to the fame of the Spanish family of statesmen and thinkers.

ABZUG (O) This word means "copy-sheet," "proof-sheet," and is taken from the printing trade.

ACKERMAN (O) A plowman.

ADELMAN (S) Adel is a variant form of Edel, as is Adele and Ethel, and all have the meaning "noble," in German. Adelman means "husband of Adel."

ADELSON (M) Son of Adel. Another form is Edelson.

ADELSTEIN (F) *or* (M) *or* (O) Adelstein means "precious stone," in German, and was probably one of the very "expensive" names for which the naming authorities exacted a high price. The name may also be an extended form of the matronym Adel(e). Finally, the name may have been assumed by a dealer in precious stones.

ADLER (H) There were actually two houses in Frankfurt with the sign of the eagle *(Adler)*, No. 27, the black eagle, and No. 86, the golden eagle.

ADONOILOM (F) A number of Galician families selected this name, which is a popular hymn in the prayer book.

AHL (O) From the German *Ahle*, "awl," a name taken by a shoemaker.

ALBUM (D) Latin for "white," a translation of Weiss.

ALEMBIK (O) Alembic is an apparatus of glass or metal formerly used in distilling. The name was taken by a distiller.

ALKUS, ALGUS (G) From Elkish, the Yiddish for Olkusz, a town in Poland.

ALPER, ALPERT (G) A truncated version of Halpern, which is itself a garbled version of Heilbronn, a German city.

ALTFELD (G) The Yiddish translation for Staropole, in Poland, which means "old field."

ALTNEU (G) A name assumed by Jews of Prague and referring to the Altneu synagogue. The synagogue is so-called because it has an older section and a newer addition. Jews, however, associated a legend with this name. They believed that the first Jews had come to Prague immediately after the fall of the Temple in the year 70. They built the synagogue only *al tenai* (which became Altneu), "on condition" that they remain there until they return to the Holy Land.

ALTSCHUL, ALTSCHULER (G) Jewish tradition associates this name, which means "old synagogue," with refugees who fled from Provence in the early fourteenth century and settled in Prague. They had paid a large sum of money to the king to be allowed to take their synagogue with them, and they brought it piece by piece. After the expulsion of the Jews in 1542 many of the Altschuls settled in Poland, Lithuania, and Russia. Not all Altschuls are descendants of the settlers of Prague. As often happened with distinguished Jewish names, they were copied and imitated by many others.

AMDUR, AMDURSKY (G) From the town of Indura in the Grodno District of Lithuania, called Amdur or Amter in Yiddish.

AMSEL, AMSLER (H) *or* (G) German Jews may derive the name from the Frankfurt ghetto house No. 21, which had the sign of the blackbird *(Amsel)*. Eastern Jews derive the name from Namslau, in Silesia. Jews called Namslau Amsle, and this was later changed to Amsel.

AMSTER (D) From the word meaning "hamster." A name given to a diligent, industrious individual.

ANDRUSSIER (G) From Andruszowce, a town in Lithuania.

ANIXTER, ONIXT (G) From Onikszty, a town in Lithuania.

ANSBACH (G) From Ansbach, a town in Bavaria.

ANTMAN (O) "Handy-man," one who works with his hands.

ANZIEHER (O) "Shoehorn" or "boot pull," in German. In Polish the form is Ancier. The name was taken by a shoemaker or a shoe merchant.

APELOWITZ (G) From Opole, a town in Poland.

APT, APTER (G) Apte or Apt is the Yiddish form of Opatow, a town in Galicia.

ARFA (O) The Polish word for a tool used to separate the chaff from the grain. Name assumed by a grain merchant.

ARKULES (P) Arke is a popular diminutive for Aaron, and Arkules is another form of Arke.

ARONIN (P) *or* (L) It either means son of Aaron or was a name assumed by a *kohen* to signify that he was a descendant of Aaron.

ARONOFF, ARONOW (P) *or* (L) Same as Aronin.

ASHKENAZ, ASHKENAZI (G) Ashkenaz is mentioned in the Bible (Genesis 10:3; Jeremiah 51:27; 1 Chronicles 1:6) and is probably Ash-ku-za in the ancient Assyrian empire. It is also identified in the early rabbinic sources as Asia. Beginning with the ninth century, however, Ashkenaz is identified with Germany and Ashkenaz and Ashkenazi mean "German." The name appears in the forms Askenazy, Asknasy, Askanasi, Esknazy, and Schinasi.

   In the seventeenth century Turkish Jews invited Jews from Austria, Hungary, Germany, and Czechoslavakia to come and settle among them. These European Jews were called Ashkenazi (coming from the German territories). When they later returned to Europe they kept the name or sometimes changed it to Deutch ("German," in German).

ASPIS (O) The Yiddish form of the Talmudic word *ushpiz,* which means a lodging or an inn. The name was assumed by the owner of an inn.

ASTRUC (P) In Provençal it means "born under a lucky star," and is the equivalent for the Hebrew names Mazal Tov or Gad. A similar Latin name Asterius appears on Jewish catacombs in Rome. Astruc first appears as a personal name in southern France in the eleventh century and eventually became a family name.

ATLIN (M) A descendant of Adele or Ethel (both names mean "noble").

AUERBACH (G) From the village of Auerbach, in Hesse-Darmstadt, Germany. The name occurs as early as the fifteenth century. Moses Auerbach, the court Jew of the bishop of Regensburg, was the first to use it. It appears on monuments in the cemetery of Vienna from 1606 on. Other forms are Awerbach, Awerbuch, Orbach, Urbach.

AUSLANDER (D) One who came from another country.

AUSPITZ (G) From Auspitz, Moravia.

AUSTERN (P) When a man whose name or whose father's name was Pesah (Passover) appeared before the Austrian officials, they often insisted that he select a German name. He solved the problem by taking the name Austern which is a garbled version of the German *Ostern*, which means Easter. Even today a number of Jews refer to Passover as the Jewish Easter.

AVIGDOR (P) The name appears in 1 Chronicles 4:4 and 4:18 but became popular because the Midrash (Leviticus Rabbah 1) states that Avigdor is one of the names of Moses. It was also phonetically associated with the Latin name Victor. Other forms of this name are Vigder, Vigdorchik ("little Victor") and Vigdorowitz ("descendant of Vigdor").

AVRECH, AVERIK, AFRICK (A) *or* (P) The word *avrekh* appears as a tribute to Joseph (Genesis 41:43). A rabbinic interpretation reads the word as an acronym for av b*ehokhmah* r*akh* b*eshanim*, "old in wisdom and tender in years." Perhaps this name was assumed by a person called Joseph in reference to his Biblical namesake.

AXELROD (P) Originally a first name appearing in the Middle Ages.

Variant forms are Axelrad, Axeldar, Axelrood, Achselrad. Some explain the name as an inverted form of Alexander. Others see it as the German name Axel with various elaborations. Another explanation offered is that the name means "shoulder" and "wheel" *(Achsel* and *Rad,* in German), and is a reference to the circular badge that Jews were forced to wear on their shoulders. While all these theories are interesting, they do not seem to offer a clear answer.

BACHRACH (G) From Bacharach, a town on the Rhine. The name appears as early as the thirteenth century. Other forms are Bacharach, Bacherach, Bacher, Bachrich.

BADANES, BODANIS (M) From Badane, the Yiddish version of the Ukrainian name Bogdana, "God-given," "beloved."

BAKST, BAXT (G) From Bakst, a town in Lithuania.

BALSAM (O) Ointment or perfume. Name taken by an apothecary.

BALTA, BALTER (G) From Balta, a town in Moldavia, where Jews took refuge during pogroms. Became part of Russia in 1791.

BAMBERG, BAMBERGER (G) From Bamberg, a town in Bavaria.

BANET, PANET (P) Bonet is the *kinnui* of Yom Tov ("holy day," "good day"), found among Jews of Provence and Spain as early as the eleventh century (it becomes Bongjorn/Bonet). The name spread to France and even into England. When the Jews were expelled from France in 1395 many families fled to Austria and Germany and later to Bohemia. The French Bonet also appears as Banet, Baneth, Panet, and Paneth.

BARBAKOFF (A) *and* (P) *and* (L) An acronym for b*en* r*eb* B*arukh* k*ohen,* son of Baruch the priest, plus the suffix -*off.*

BARDACH (A) *and* (P) B*en* r*eb* D*avid* h*arif,* "son of David the brilliant mind."

BARON (P) *and/or* (L) A form of *bar aron* ("son of Aaron"), telescoped into one word; it indicates priestly descent.

BARR *or* BAR (G) From the town of Bar in the Ukraine. The town was the property of Bona Sforza, sixteenth-century queen of Poland, who was born in Bari, Italy. Jewish girls in that town were named Bona in honor of the queen, and this name often became Bina, in Yiddish.

BARU (A) *and* (P) B*en reb* Wolff ("son of Wolff").

BASKIND, BASKIN (M) Basyah (Batyah) becomes Bashe in Yiddish. Baskin is a matronymic: Bas (for Bashe or Basheva) plus *-kin*, the Russian patronymic suffix. Later on, someone in the family who was unfamiliar with the Russian ending changed the *kin* to *kind*. This happens very often in names ending with *kin*.

BASS (O) A translation of the Hebrew for singer.

BAUM (O) Although the word is "tree" in German, the name has nothing to do with a tree. It is a shortened form for *Schlagbaum*, the tollgate on a highway or road.

BAUMGARTEN (G) "Orchard," in German. A name assumed by one living near an orchard.

BECHOR (P) A name given to the first-born son among Sephardim. Other forms are Bechar, Beshar.

BECHTHEIM (G) Bechtheim, a town in Hesse, Germany.

BECKMAN (A) *or* (O) As a non-Jewish name, Beckman means "baker" and a small number of Jews who were bakers adopted it. However, in most cases, as a Jewish name, it is an acronym for b*ene* k*edoshim* (Beck) plus the elaborated *-mann*.

BEDWINEK (O) A Polish word which means "a traveling merchant or peddler." It is associated with Bedouin. An itinerant merchant assumed this name.

BEHAR (A) *or* (G) Among western and eastern European Jews Behar is an acronym for b*en* har*av*, "the son of the rabbi." If it is a Sephardic name, it is derived from the Arabic and means "from the sea."

BEIFUSS (P) Although the word *Beifuss* is German for the aromatic herb, the name is really an inverted form of Veivis, Feivis ("life").

BEILIN, BAILIN (M) A name derived from Beile, Bayla, the Yiddish version of the Italian Bella ("beautiful"). The final "n" represents -*in*, the Slavic patronymic suffix.

BELKIN (M) Bella or its Yiddish equivalent Bayla becomes the diminutive Belka or Beilke. The final "n" is the Slavic suffix -*in* indicating descent. Sometimes Belkin is elaborated into Belkind.

BELMONT, BELMONTE (G) A German family that traces its descent to a Portuguese-Dutch Marrano family from Belmonte on the Iberian Peninsula. King Manuel of Portugal gave the name and the city to the family.

BELOFSKY, BELLOW (G) From Belev, a town in Russia.

BENDER (G) *or* (O) Either from Bender, a small town in Rumania or from the German *Bender*, which means "cooper" or "cask maker."

BENOWITZ (P) Ber becomes Benno in Czech or Polish diminutives. The name means "son of Ber" (the *kinnui* of Issachar).

BENSHEIM (G) A town in Hesse, Germany.

BENSINGER (G) From Benzingen, a town in Baden Wurttemburg, Germany.

BENTWICH (G) From Bentwisch, the name of several localities in Germany.

BERGER (G) *or* (P) As a place of origin Berger means "one coming from Berg," a hilly place. As a patronymic, Galician Jews often transformed the Hebrew Barukh into Berger, Berg, or Bergman.

BERKAL (G) A Yiddish version of Perkallen, a locality in what was formerly Prussia.

BERKMAN (P) A form of Berko which is a form of Ber, the *kinnui* of Issachar.

BERKO, BERKOWITZ (P) The name Berko is the *kinnui* of Issachar. Berkowitz originated in Brody in the middle of the eighteenth century and means "the son of Berko." When Poland was partitioned among Prussia, Russia, and Austria, the Berkowitz branch of the family retained its name, and the Austrian branch took the name Bernstein.

BERNICK (G) From Berniki, a town in Poland.

BERNSTEIN (P) *or* (O) *Bernstein* is German for "amber." Some Bernsteins may have derived their name from their dealings in amber. However, almost all the Bernsteins are descendants of a person called Berko or Berish, a diminutive for Ber, the *kinnui* for Issachar.

BERTINERO (G) A town in north Italy.

BESSER (O) From Besserer, the title of a German officer of the court who levied fines. As a Jewish name, it indicates either the tax collector of the Jewish community or a rabbinic judge.

BETTELHEIM (D) A Hungarian Jewish family name. It is a corruption of Bethlen Jude, the Jew involved with Bethlen and refers to an incident where a Jew fought for his wife's honor and vanquished her abductor, a certain Count Bethlen.

BETTSACK (P) *or* (A) *or* (O) A garbled version of Pesah. Or the acronym for b*en* t*ehorim* z*era* k*edoshim*, "a son of pure lineage, a descendant of martyrs." Or it may be phonetically associated with Bettsack, the German for mattress and indicate a dealer in, or maker of, mattresses.

BIBACK, BIBICK (O) From the Russian and Polish *bibika (bibik,* in Yiddish), the Harmel plant from which a red dye is derived. The name was assumed by one in the dyeing trade. Jews have been in the occupation of dyeing since ancient times.

BICKEL (O) *or* (A) Either from *Bickel,* the German for pick-axe and denotes someone who used this tool in his work. Or an acronym for bene yisrael kedoshim leadonai "the children of Israel are holy unto God."

BIEDERMAN (D) "Honest man." Other form is Beederman.

BILDHAUER (P) or (O) Bildhauer is the German for "sculptor" and may refer to someone with that skill. However, the name was usually assumed by one whose Hebrew name was Betzalel, the Biblical artisan who built the Tabernacle.

BINDER (O) Either a bookbinder (Buchbinder, in German) or a cooper (Fassbinder, in German). Another form of the name is Bindler.

BING (G) From Bingen, Hesse, Germany.

BIRNBAUM (H) or (G) or (P) The most common derivation is from the Frankfurt ghetto house No. 167 that had the sign of a pear tree (Birnbaum). There is also a town named Birnbaum in the Prussian-Polish province of Posen and about 10 percent of the Jewish Birnbaums come from there. Finally, some Jews with the name Ber selected Birnbaum, which is sometimes rendered as Berenbaum.

BISTRITZKY (G) From Bistritz, a town in Hungary. The town was called Bistrita in Rumanian and Beszterce in Hungarian.

BITENSKY (G) From Biten, a town in Russia.

BLACHER (O) A tinsmith or a dealer in tin ware.

BLASER (O) Sounding the ram's horn is an important ritual in the synagogue, and the one who performs this ritual is called the shofer-blozer, in Yiddish, or just blozer or blaser. It is retained in the name Blaser or Blazer.

BLASHKI, BLASZKA (G) From Blaszki, a town in Poland.

BLAU (A) or (D) or (F) Blau often stands for ben leadoni avi, which means "son of my father and master," a common signature used by sons of rabbis. Blau also means "blue," "light-complexioned," "blonde," and may have described a person's appearance. Finally, in many Hungarian communities the people were divided into arbitrary categories for the purpose of assigning them names. The most common categories were Weiss, ("white"), Schwartz ("black"), Gross ("big"), Klein ("little"). Sometimes Blau ("blue") and Roth ("red") were added for good measure.

BLAUSTEIN (A) *or* (D) *or* (F) *or* (O) The name could be Blau with the added -*stein* for elaboration. It could also signify a dealer in antimony, which is used in dyes and medicines. Antimony is called "blue stone," *Blaustein.*

BLECHMAN, BLECHER (O) "Tinsmith," in German.

BLEICH (D) *or* (O) "Pale," in German. A person with a pale complexion or one who is a bleacher of textiles.

BLEIER (O) One who smelts lead.

BLEIWEISS (O) *or* (D) *Bleiweiss* means "white lead," in German. This ingredient was used in paint and plaster, and the name means the seller of these items. Or it may be a person with a very white complexion.

BLITSTEIN (F) At first glance this word seems to be associated with the idea of lightning and stone, but actually it is the Yiddish for "blood stone," a mineral called hematite to which folk-lore ascribed all kinds of good fortune. The ancient Egyptians and Greeks and later the people of the Middle Ages believed that it would stop bleeding, and that it was an aid to longevity and the preservation of youthful vigor. In medieval France it was associated with the legend of the Wandering Jew, who was supposed to sell or give away such stones. In World War I many German soldiers wore necklaces of bloodstones for protection.

BLOCH (G) From the Slavic *vlach*, "foreigner." The name originated when Jews from central Europe migrated into Poland and were given the name. When they returned to German areas, the name was Germanized into Bloch.

BLOOM (M) *or* (H) See Blum.

BLOOMFIELD (M) *or* (H) This is a translation of Blumfeld or Blumenfeld, which is an extension and variant of Blum.

BLOWITZ (G) From Blowitz, a town in Bohemia.

BLUM (M) *or* (H) Although some Blums come from the house sign in Frankfurt which depicted a flower, the vast majority of Blums derive their name from the feminine name Bluma. Although it is popularly accepted as coming from *Blume* (German for "flower"), Blum really is a garbled version of the Spanish *Paloma*, "dove." Other extensions of this name are Blumenberg, Blumenfeld, Blumengarten, Blumenheim, Blumenkrantz, Blumenkrohn, Blumenreich, Blumenstein, Blumenstock, Blumenthal, Blumkin. Even though there are almost a dozen communities in Germany named Blumberg, the Jewish family name does not come from these locations but also from the extension of *Blume*. At the time names were assumed it was quite fashionable to make them long; this was considered more elegant and in good taste—hence the addition of -*stein*, -*thal*, -*reich*, -*feld*, -*heim*, etc. Today, our tastes are toward simpler and shorter forms.

BLUSTEIN (A) Although the name sounds like the German or Yiddish "blue stone," its derivation is the acronym for the expression b*en* l*eadoni* a*vi*, "the son of my revered father." Sons of rabbis often signed their name this way in correspondence or books. The -*stein* is sometimes replaced by -*shein* and these suffixes are for the purpose of extending the name.

BOBROFF (G) From Bobrov, a town in Russia.

BODENSTEIN (G) The name of several places in different areas of Germany.

BODNER (O) The Yiddish form of the Polish Bednarz, "cooper" or "barrel maker."

BOERNE (P) The Hebrew *barukh*, "blessed," was sometimes changed into the German Boerne.

BOGATCH (D) From the Polish "rich."

BOGATI (D) From the Russian "rich."

BOGOLUB (P) The Slavic translation of Gottlieb, which is the German-Yiddish of Yedidiah, "beloved of God."

BOLOTIN (G) The Slavic *bloto* ("mud") is included in a large number of towns and villages all over Poland and Russia such as Blotno or Blotnia. The name Bolotin is derived from these places.

BORER (O) Although the name sounds like the German *Bohrer*, "drill," "bore," it has nothing to do with any occupation using that tool. It is, rather, a title of honor to distinguished individuals in the community who served as the electors and participated in the selection of the head of the community. Borer in Hebrew means "one who chooses."

BORNSTEIN (P) *or* (O) A variant of Bernstein. Since Hebrew and Yiddish were written without vowels, a name could assume various forms.

BORODATY (D) "Bearded," in Russian. It was conferred by officials upon Jews. Since all eastern European Jews wore beards, the name was rather widespread.

BOROS (O) In Hungarian this name means "one who ferments and sells wine."

BOROWSKY (G) One who lived in a small wooded area.

BORTNIK (G) From the village of Bortniki in Russia. It means "bee-keepers."

BORUCHSCHOMER (F) This is the name of the opening prayer of the morning service. It was either selected as an invention or perhaps a Jew opened the prayer book when he needed a name and choose the first word that appeared.

BOTNICK (O) Polish Jews who manufactured ladies shoes *(botinka)* adopted this name. Russian Jews who made tubs, troughs, pails, etc., adopted the name Batnik. The transformation from final "k" to "ck" is German influence.

BOTUSHANSKY (G) From Botosani, a town in Rumania that is called Botoshan in Yiddish.

BOTWINNIK (G) A nickname for one who was born in Lithuania.

BOXERMAN (O) One who sold St. John's bread, which in Yiddish is called *bokser* and was known in German as *Bockshorn*. This food was especially popular on the Fifteenth Day of Shevat.

BRAGIN (G) From Bragin, a town in White Russia.

BRAND (A) *or* (O) It can stand for b*en reb* Nachman David, "son of Nachman David." It could also refer to a distiller, a *Brandler*, in German.

BRANDEIS (G) From the town of Brandeis, in Bohemia, where Jews from Germany first settled in 1440. The name appears in the form of Brandes and Brandys, Brandiss, and among Russian Jews it is spelled Barondes.

BRANDER, BRENDER (O) The German name for the alembic apparatus of distilling. The name was taken by a distiller.

BRANDLER (O) The production of alcohol was a government monopoly, and the privilege to engage in this trade was leased to individuals who enjoyed a certain status in the community. Brandler is the name for such a distiller.

BRAUDE (G) Another version of the Galician town of Brody, an important center of Jewish life on the border between Austria and Russia. Other forms of the name are Broder, Brod, Brodt, Brodsky, Brady, and Brewda. There is another Brod, in Moravia, and some Jews have derived the name from there. In Russian and Polish Brody means "ford," a shallow place in a river.

BRAVERMAN (O) A brewer.

BREGER (O) A variant pronunciation of the German *Breuer,* "brewer."

BREINDEL (M) A number of names were fashioned in tribute to a matriarch in the family named Breine or Breindel. Such names as Braunfeld, Braunschild, Braunspan, Braunstein, Braunthal, Brandelstein.

BREYER (O) Breyer and Breier are other forms for brewer.

BRILL (A) *or* (G) Most Brills derive the name from the acronym b*en reb* Yehudah *L*ayb, but some come from Bruel in western Germany.

BRILLIANT (O) Brilliant is a cut diamond and in Yiddish means a very expensive diamond. This would be a name for a dealer in precious stones.

BROITMAN (O) "Bread man," in Yiddish. Name assumed by a baker.

BROMBERG (G) Bromberg is now Bydgoszcz, a town in Poland.

BRONFMAN (O) *Bronfn* is the Yiddish for the German *Branntwein,* "spirits," "whiskey." The name was originally Bronfen-man, the man who made or sold whiskey.

BRONSTEIN A variant form of Braunstein.

BROSTOFF (G) From Brzostowica, a town in Poland.

BRUCKENSTEIN (P) Bruckenstein, Bruckstein, and Brickenstein are phonetically related to the word *Bruk (brik)*, which is the Yiddish for pavement. The name, however, has no connection with paving stones. It is the name for Barukh. Since the authorities frowned on Hebrew family names, the name Barukh was disguised in the forms above.

BUFMAN (O) This is a name adapted from the Slavic for jester or wag. It was a name assumed by a *badhan*, the traditional entertainer at Jewish weddings.

BUKSZPAN (O) The Polish word for *Buxbaum* ("box tree") is Bukszpan. Boxwood was important for artistic carving and woodworking, and a worker with boxwood assumed this name.

BULKA (O) "Roll," in Polish. The name was assumed by a baker.

BURACK (O) A dealer in beets.

BURLA (O) In Ladino, Burla means "onyx." The name was adopted by Jews in the jewelry trade.

BURSTEIN (G) From Bursztyn, a town in Poland.

BUXBAUM (G) *or* (O) *or* (H) German Jews selected this name either from the Frankfurt house sign No. 169 or from the fact that box trees grew in their vicinity. Galician Jews selected this name when they worked with boxwood. The name also appears as Buchsbaum.

CALISCH (KALISCH) (G) *or* (O) From Kalisz, a town in Poland, or from *kalich*, the Yiddish for "lime." A dealer in lime.

CASSIRER (O) *Kassirer* is the Yiddish-German for "cashier" and was the title of the collector of taxes in the community.

CASUTO (D) From *casato*, "family," in Italian. This Italian family felt so distinguished that they considered no other distinction necessary.

CHABAS (A) *and* (C) H*asan* B*arukh* s*ofer*, "son-in-law of Barukh the scribe."

CHABIN (G) From Chabne, a town in the Ukraine. Other forms of the name are Chabner, Chubinsky, Chubin.

CHAIT (O) From Hebrew *hayat*, "tailor."

CHALEF (O) The *halef* was the knife used by a *shohet*.

CHAMUDES (P) A name assumed by one called Daniel and based on the Biblical reference in Daniel 9:23, where he is called "beloved" (*hamudot*, in Hebrew). Other variations are Chameides, Chamedes, Chamides.

CHANKIN (M) From the name Chana (Hana), plus -*kin*, the Russian suffix indicating descent. Other forms of this matronymic are Chanen, Chanin, Hankin, Henkin.

CHARNESS, CHARNIS (M) *or* (C) Either from *charna* ("dark," in

Slavic) or standing for h*asan* r*eb* N*atan* s*ofer*, "son-in-law of Nathan the scribe."

CHARRIK (A) *and* (C) H*asan* r*eb* Yosef *K*alman, "son-in-law of Yosef Kalman."

CHARRY (A) *and* (C) H*asan* r*eb* Yosef "son-in-law of Yosef."

CHASIN, CHASINS, CHASON (O) Chasin is the transliteration of the Hebrew *hazan*, "cantor."

CHERNIAK, CHERNIK (O) Cherniak is Slavic for "cuttlefish," the source of a black secretion from which the pigment sepia is made. The bearer of the name either sold sepia, used it in writing, or dispensed it as a medicine.

CHERNOFF, CHERNOFFSKY (M) A descendant of Cherna, which is a variant of Charna, Slavic for "dark."

CHIEL (P) An abbreviated form of the name Yehiel.

CHIGER (D) From the Hebrew *higger*, "lame," describing the one who first assumed the name.

CHODOSH (D) *and* (F) *Hadash* means "new" in Hebrew and the man who selected it felt that he was now a new person with a new name. Other forms are Chodesh, Chodes. A name like Neuman, Newman, or Novick are equivalents.

CHOMSKY (G) From Chomsk, a town near Pinsk in what was once Lithuania, later Poland, and now Russia.

CHUDNOW (G) From Chudnow, a town in Russia. The name often appears as Chudnovsky.

CITRON (O) One who sold lemons. *Zitrone* is "lemon" in German.

COGAN (L) A variant of Kogan, the Slavic form for Kohen, Cohen.

COLOMBO (P) Italian for the Hebrew Yonah (Jonah) "dove."

CORNFELD (G) *or* (L) Cornfeld is the anglicized spelling of Kornfeld which means "field of grain." While some Cornfelds refer to a geographic location, many of the Jewish family names which begin with the element Korn (or Corn) are really disguised forms for Kohen (Cohen). Thus, we have Cornfeld, Kornberg (Cornberg), Cornblum, Korngold, Corngreen, Corngut, Kornreich, Cornblith, Cornfein, Cornpracht.

DANTO (P) A diminutive for David.

DASKAL (DASKELOWITZ) (O) Rumanian for a cantor's assistant; the member of a choir.

DAUBE (M) *or* (H) *or* (O) Daube is a "barrel stave" in German and perhaps some Jews in that trade adopted this name. For most Jews, Daube is another form for the German *Taube*, "dove." One of the house signs in Frankfurt was the Taube. In the Middle Ages a popular first name for women was Taube, which in Yiddish took the form Teibel.

DAUBER (P) *or* (O) A form of Tauber or Taub ("dove," in German), which is the translation of the name Yonah (Jonah). Or a seller of pigeons.

DAVIS (P) Davis is an English name which means "son of David." Some Jews in English-speaking countries assumed this patronymic form.

DEKOVNICK (O) From the Polish *dekownik*, "a maker of straw roofs."

DEMBITZ (G) From Debica (pronounced Dembitza), a town in Galicia.

DEWOSKIN (M) Descendant of Dewoska, a nickname for Devorah, (Deborah).

DICK (D) "Stout," in German.

DICKENSTEIN, DICKSTEIN (G) *or* (D) In German these words mean "stout stone," a rather uncomplimentary name bestowed by the authorities. Others take it for a place that was located near large boulders or from the locality of Duckstein which was pronounced Dickstein.

DISSEN (G) From the Polish Dzisna and the Russian Disna, a town near Vilna, Lithuania.

DOBKIN (M) Descendant of Dobe, a nickname for Devorah (Deborah).

DOBRIN (M) Dobra is the Polish translation of Gittel, which is the Yiddish for the name Bona ("good"). Girls were given the name Bona or Bina in honor of Queen Bona Sforza.

DOLINSKY (G) From Dolina, towns in Lithuania and in Galicia.

DRATWA (O) Dratwa is Polish for the thread used in stitching shoes and boots. The name was selected by a shoemaker.

DRECHSLER (O) "Turner," in German, one who fashioned objects on a lathe. Variants are Dressler, Drexler, Drexsler.

DREEBIN (G) From Drybin, a town in the Ukraine.

DREYFUSS (G) Variants are Dreifuss, Trefus, Trevis, Trivash, Tribas. Treves appears as early as the fourteenth century.

DRUCKER (O) "Printer," in German.

DUBIN (G) From Dubina, a town in Lithuania. It means "area of oak trees."

DUBOW (G) In Russian, Ukrainian, and Polish, "a place of oak trees." Variants of the name are Dubowsky and Dubofsky.

DUCHOVNY (O) *or* (L) Duchovny is Russian for clergyman. The name was given either to a rabbi or to a *kohen* (priest).

DUNKELMAN (D) An old German word for "a deeply religious man."

DURCHSCHLAG (O) *or* (P) "Strainer," "sieve," in German. It may have to do with an occupation that involved this utensil. Some associate Durchschlag as a garbled version of Dargoslav, an old Slavic name that means "a man who cherishes glory."

DUSHKIN, DUSKIN (M) Descended from Dushe or Dushke, a nickname for Devorah (Deborah).

DVORETZ (G) A town in the area of Grodno.

ECKSTEIN (F) Eckstein means "a cornerstone" and is a reference to Psalm 118:22; "The stone that the builders rejected has become a cornerstone." This has been traditionally viewed as a reference to the tragic fate of Israel and expressed the hope that in the future its fortune would rise.

EDELMAN (S) The name means: "husband of Edel." Often a Jewish family name is associated with the wife's name in cases where she was the breadwinner or where she came from the more distinguished family lineage *(yichus)*.

EDELSTEIN (F) *or* (M) *or* (O) The name means "precious stone" and was probably one of the very "expensive" names purchased from the authorities. It could also be an extended form of the feminine Edel. Another variant is Edelsberg. Finally, the name may have been assumed by one who dealt with precious stones.

EGER (G) From Eger, a town in western Bohemia. Other forms are Egers and Eiger.

EHMANN (D) "Husband," in German. In many communities no marriage licenses were granted until military service was completed. As a result, many Jews were married by the rabbi only, and their marriages were never officially registered. This name was selected by one who could officially be registered as a "husband," and indicated that all the military requirements were met.

EHRENTREU (P) *or* (L) This name in German means "faithful to honor," but almost all Jewish names with Ehren have no connection with the German word for honor. They are disguised forms for Aaron or for a *kohen* (one descended from Aaron the high priest).

EHRLICH (P) *and* (F) *or* (L) Although the word means "honest" in German, it was adopted because of its phonetic value. Jews called Aaron selected this name because it was close enough to Aaron in sound and Germanic enough to pass the naming officials. Variations include Ehrman, Ehrenfreund,

Ehrenpreis, Ehrenhaft, Ehrenfrucht, Ehrenstein, Ehrenberg, Ehrenhaus, Ehrenfeld, Ehrenfest, Ehrenfried, Ehrenkrantz, Ehrenreich, Ehrenteil, Ehrenthal, Ehrenzweig, Ehrenstamm, etc. As with all names referring to Aaron, the reference may be to an immediate ancestor or to the Biblical Aaron, thus indicating priestly lineage.

EIBENSCHITZ (G) A city in South Moravia, also known as Ivančice. Variations of the family name are Eibeschütz, Eibenschütz, Eybeschitz.

EICHHORN (G) *or* (H) Eichhorn or Eichorn is the German for "squirrel" and this word has been incorporated into the name of a number of places where squirrels are found. It may also refer to a house or street or landmark where there was a sign of the squirrel.

EIFERMAN (G) The name seems to mean "man of zeal" in German, but as a Jewish family name it has nothing to do with that definition. Jews from Prague or Burgenland who had called themselves Ash or Asch, the acronym for Altschul or Ayzenschtat (Eisenstadt), translated their name to Efer, which is the Hebrew for "ashes" (Ash). Efer became Germanized to Eifer, and the man of Ash (Eferman) became Eiferman.

EIGES (M) Eige is an abbreviation of Feige, an old German word for "violet." The word has been incorrectly associated with the Yiddish "bird."

EINSTEIN (O) From a German word which means "to enclose with stone." The name was assumed by a mason.

EISEMAN, EISEMANN (P) A pet name for Isaac was Eise, which was expanded to Eiseman or Eisenman.

EISENBERG (G) *or* (P) There is a town called Eisenberg (Eisenburg) in the Hungarian district of Vas and another Eisenburg in Thuringia. A number of Jews selected these place names for their family names. However, very often a Jewish family name that contains the element of Eisen ("iron," in German) is really a veiled reference to Isaac (Eizik, often called Eise).

As a result we have the following variants on the patronym Isaac: Eisenman, Eisman, Eisengarten, Eisenstein, Eisenstam, Eisenkraft, Eisenstark, and Eisenbach.

EISNER (P) The pet name for Isaac, Eise, was extended to Eisner, Eisinger, Eisler.

ELIAS (P) Elias is the form for Elijah which appears in the Greek translation of the Bible. It has passed into a number of languages in this version.

EMALE (O) From *Emalja*, Polish for "enamel ware." A dealer in enamel ware.

EMBDEN (EMDEN) (G) From Emden, a town in the province of Hannover, Germany.

ENKER (F) Enker also appears in the form Anker which is the German word for "anchor." The anchor was a symbol of hope and salvation and was often used as a good luck sign on homes and business establishments. It was selected as a family name for the same reason.

ENTIN (M) Entin means "descended from Ente." Ente is a variant pronunciation for the feminine Yente.

EPHRON (P) Although in the Bible Ephron is the name of a Hittite, the Jewish family name Ephron is a garbled version of Ephrom and is derived from Ephraim. Since the "f" ("ph") and "v" represent interchangeable sounds the name also appears as Evron.

EPHROS (F) This is the name of a place near Bethlehem where Rachel was buried (Genesis 48:7). It is also the name of Caleb's wife (1 Chronicles 2:19). While Ephros (Ephrat in Sephardic Hebrew) is very popular as a name for girls in Israel today, we have no tradition of its usage in earlier years, except for the reference in the Bible. We must, therefore, assume that the name was selected as a family name for some personal reason to which we are not privy.

EPSTEIN (G) This is one of the oldest Jewish family names and appears as early as 1392. There is an Eppstein in Bavaria, an

Eppstein in Hesse, and an Ebstein in Styria, Austria. Of special interest is the Styrian family. In 1492 a family called Benveniste was expelled from Spain. One branch went to Turkey and maintained its Spanish name; a second branch came to Ebstein in Styria, Austria. This family were Levites, and Ebstein ultimately became Epstein. The name appears as Epsteen, Eppenstein, and in several other variations. During the course of the centuries the name was assumed by many people, not because of any relationship, but because it was so well known.

ERLANGER (G) From Erlangen, a town in Bavaria.

ESTERSON (M) Son of Esther.

ESTRIN (M) Descended from Esther.

ETTINGER (G) From Oettingen, a town in Bavaria. The name sometimes appears as Oettinger.

ETTLINGER (G) From Ettlingen, a town in Baden.

FALK (H) *or* (P) *or* (A) House No. 62 in Frankfurt bore the sign of the *Falke*, "falcon" or "hawk," and some Falks derive their name from that source. In addition, Jews called Joshua (Yehoshua) adopted Falk as the *kinnui* in the forms of Falk, Valk, Walk, Wallik, Wallich. However, we are not certain as to whether these mean "falcon," since the association of Joshua and falcon is not clear. (One researcher states that just as the falcon circles its prey, so Joshua circled and explored the Holy Land before swooping down upon it. This is an amusing, but rather far-fetched explanation.) Finally, some derive Valk from an acronym of *veahavta lereakha kamokha*, "love thy neighbor as thyself." Variations of Falk are Falkheim, Falkenberg, Falkenfeld, Falkenheim, Falkenstein, Falkenthal.

FARKAS (P) The Hungarian for "wolf," the *kinnui* for Benjamin.

FEDER (O) *Feder* is a quill in German and Yiddish and the name was taken by a scribe. Another form is Federman.

FEDERBUSCH (O) Federbusch means "plumed crest" used in women's hats and was assumed by a dealer in aigrette.

FEIGE (M) Feige is really derived from Veigelchen or Veigelein which means "violet," in German. These changed phonetically to Feige or Feigel, and were misunderstood as "fig" or "bird," in Yiddish. As a result there developed many variations of the matronym: Feig, Feigel, Figel, Feigelstock, Feilchenfeld, Fogel, Vogel, Fogelman, Fogelson, Fogelstein, Fogelsdorf, Fogelbaum, Fogelsang, Fagan, Fagin, Feigin, Feigon, Feigenblat, Feigenbaum, Feigler, Feigelman, Figlin, Figler, etc.

FEINBERG (G) *or* (O) Since the "f" and "v" are interchanged, Feinberg is really Veinberg, the pronunciation of Weinberg in Silesia. Sometimes Weinberg was assumed by people in the wine business.

FEINER (O) Feiner is really Weiner, a dealer of producer or wine.

FEINGOLD, FEINSILVER (O) These are names adopted by a dealer in silver and gold.

FEINSTEIN (O) The name means "fine stone" and was assumed by one who dealt in precious stones, gold, and silver—a jeweler. Feinstein may also be a version of Weinstein and this would refer to a wine dealer.

FEKETE (D) Fekete is Hungarian for "black." When Hungarian Jews had to assume permanent family names the authorities often assembled the local Jews in the town square, divided them into four groups—dark-haired, light-haired, tall, and short. They were then named Schwartz ("black"), Weiss ("white"), Gross ("tall"), and Klein ("short"). A Schwartz translated his name into Fekete.

FELLER (O) *Fell* means "hide" or "skin" in German and in Yiddish. Jews were in the hide trade for many years as the following names indicated: Feller, Fellerman, Fellner, Felman, Felltrager, Filler.

FENSTER (O) Fenster means "a window" in Yiddish and German. A seller or producer of windows and doors assumed this name.

FERBER (O) A variant of Farber, a dyer of cloth or a stainer of hides.

FETTERER (O) A feather merchant.

FEUCHTWANGER (G) From Feuchtwangen, a town in Franconia.

FEUER (P) A name selected by one called Uri or Meir, signifying light or fire in German.

FILEHNE (G) From Filehne, a town in Posen.

FINE (D) *or* (O) Fine is the English for Fein which means "fine" and is part of the descriptive Feinermann, "nice, fine person." Or "fein" could be a variant of Wein, making the bearer a wine merchant.

FINK (D) *or* (M) *or* (P) *or* (O) Fink is the German for "finch" and may be a descriptive word for a person who is small and active. But the Jewish family name Fink may be a matronym. Finkel was a very popular woman's name in medieval Germany. Another woman's name was Pinke which (by exchange of "p" and "f," identical letters in Hebrew and Yiddish) was also read Finke. Sometimes the man's name Pinhas appears as a variant Fink. As a family name, Fink is extended into Finkenfeld, Finkerfeld, Finkheim, Finkhof, Finkdorf, Finkelstein. This last form could also refer to a dealer in precious gems, because Finkelstein is the old German word for "diamond."

FINKELSTEIN (F) *or* (M) The Yiddish for pyrite, a mineral which, according to folklore, brought good luck and was, therefore, selected as a family name. A second possibility is that it is a matronym from Finkel, a popular name for Jewish women in medieval Germany.

FINN (D) From *fin*, Polish for "wise, clever, quick-witted."

FIRESTONE (G) *or* (O) At the border between Galicia and the Czechoslovakian province of Zips is a mountain called Fuzko, which in German is called Feuerstein. This mountain is a well-known landmark, visible on both sides of the border.

Many Jews in the area took its name as their family name. Feuerstein is also the German word for "flint," and before the invention of modern matches flint-making was an important Jewish industry in central Europe. Some Feuersteins may have originated as occupational names. Firestone is, of course, the English translation.

FISCHBEIN (O) Fischbein is the German for "whalebone," an item used for making many things.

FISHKIN, FISHKIND (P) This name is the *kinnui* of Ephraim, plus the Slavic suffix -*kin*, denoting descent. The suffix was later extended to "kind." If Fish is the *kinnui* of Yeruham, then it has nothing to do with fish but is really from Vish, a form of the word meaning life.

FLAXMAN (O) *or* (D) Flaxman is a trade name that denotes a dealer in flax, flaxseed oil, or hemp. Or it may refer to the color of a person's hair. Other variations of the name are Flacksman, Flax, Flaks, Flexner.

FLEISCHHAKER, FLEISCHHAUER, FLEISCHMAN (O) Fleischhaker means "cleaver" or "meat chopper." Fleischhauer means "meat cutter" and Fleischman means "meat man," in German. All these names were assumed by butchers.

FLEISCHER (O) It is the German word for "butcher" or "meat dealer." The trade of butcher was very important in the Middle Ages. First of all, it was the source of supply of kosher meat, which was the only kind available to Jews, for religious reasons. Secondly, the butchers in the ghettos of medieval Europe were often an unofficial Jewish army and self-defense group, since they were the only ones familiar with the handling of knives and axes.

FLOSS, FLOSSER (G) From the village Floss in Bavaria, which was settled by Jewish cloth merchants. It was called "Judenberg."

FONSECA (G) From Fonseca, a town in Spain. The name means "dry spring."

FORMAN (O) Forman or Furman is the Yiddish word for "a carter" or "a teamster." Prior to the invention of railroads these teamsters were a very important source of transportation and commercial shipping all through Russia and Poland.

FORSCHEIM (G) A town near Bamberg.

FORTEL, FERTEL (G) The ghetto gates were called *fertel* in Yiddish (German, *Viertel*). This name denotes a resident near the ghetto gates.

FRADKIN (M) Named after Freide (Frayda), which means "joy." A diminutive of Frayda is Fradel or Fradke, and the final "n" is Russian, denoting descent.

FRAM (P) An adaptation of Abraham.

FRANKEL (G) Frankel originated in the province of Franken (Franconia). It first appears among non-Jews in the fourteenth century and among Jews in the sixteenth century. It was originally assumed by Jews from Franconia who settled in Vienna. After the Jews were expelled from Vienna in 1669, the Frankel family scattered all over Europe. A number of families belong to this same original family, among them: Theomim, Munk, Heller and Wallerstein, Zwillinger, Mirels, and Neumark.

FRAYDA (M) A number of derivations have been created from the matronym Frayda, which means "joy" in Yiddish-German: Freud, Freudenberg, Freudenfeld, Freudenfels, Freudenheim, Freudenstein, Freudenthal, Freudman, Freudenreich. Sometimes this name was understood as meaning "peace," and the following were derived from it: Friedheim, Friedenheim, Friedenstein, Friedenthal, Friedwald, Friedenwald, Friedson, Friedjung, Friedlich, Friedenson, and Frieder.

FREILICH, FREILACH (P) *Freylikh* in Yiddish means "happy" and is a patronym for the Hebrew Simchah.

FRIEDLAND (G) From Friedland, in Upper Silesia, or from

Markisch-Friedland, in Prussia. Another version is Friedländer, which in English becomes simply Freedland.

FRIEDMAN, FRIED (P) These names which have the idea of peace were patronyms for Shelomo (Solomon) or Shalom. There were many European countries in which it was forbidden to assume Hebrew names as family names. By selecting names like Fried or Friedman, which were perfectly good German words, the Jews could still preserve the meaning of Solomon and Shalom.

FROIKIN (P) Ephraim became abbreviated to Froim, and this became another affectionate diminutive Froike or Efroike. Froikin or Efroikin means "descendant of Ephraim."

FROMEL (P) Another adaptation of Abraham. Avraham becomes Avrum, which becomes Avromel. The "v" is pronounced as "f" in German, and Avromel becomes Vromel, which becomes Fromel. Sometimes From moved on to become Fromkin, "descendant of Afrom." In the same way the name Frommer (German for "pious person") has nothing to do with piety. It originally was Fromer, derived from Abraham, but was spelled Frommer to give it a German appearance and to serve as a cover for Abraham.

FUCHS (H) *or* (D) In the ghetto of Frankfurt, house No. 78 had the sign of the Fuchs ("fox), and a number of German Jews derive their name from that source. Among eastern European Jews the family name may stem from a nickname Fox attributed to red-headed people. Finally, rabbis in Poland in the eighteenth and nineteenth centuries wore a special garb with a fox-lined outer garment, and when names were given out this may have influenced the selection. In Poland the word for fox is *lis,* and the Jewish family name Liss or Lis is the result. In German the name is Fuchs, and in English the name is Fox.

FUDYM (O) The Yiddish *fudm* or *fudim* is "thread" and was selected by a tailor.

FULD (G) From Fulda, a town in Germany.

FUTORIAN (O) A furrier.

FUTTERMAN (O) "Furrier," in Yiddish. In German the word means "one who sold feed or fodder," but this was never the meaning of the Jewish name.

GABEL (G) Gabel or Gabler is derived from Gable, a town in Bohemia.

GALINSKY (O) One who sold quality grain.

GAMORAN (G) From Gommern, a town in Magdeburg in Westphalia.

GARBER (O) Garber, or Gerber, is "tanner" in Yiddish. Garbowsky is the Polish equivalent.

GARFUNKEL (O) *or* (F) Garfunkel is from the old German Karfunkel or Karfunkelstein which mean "diamond." The name was assumed by one who was a diamond dealer or was an expensive name bought from the naming authorities. Other derivations are: Gorfinkel, Garfinkel, and sometimes Finkelstein and Finkel are derivatives of the second part of the old German name.

GARMAIZE (G) The old Hebrew name for the city of Worms.

GARTENHAUS (G) Phonetically, this word seems to be associated with a summer house and a garden, but actually it comes from Kartuzy, a town in Galicia.

GASTER (G) The late Dr. Moses Gaster was of the opinion that his family name was a garbled version of De Castro, a widespread Sephardic name that is found in many countries of Europe, North, Central, and South America. This name is quite common among Christians of Spain and South America and is probably derived from a number of localities called Castro. The Jewish name is derived from the town of Castro near Cordova, Spain.

GEDULD (P) In present-day German, *Geduld* means "patience." However, an older German vernacular meaning is "peace." When Warsaw was occupied by the Prussians from 1794–

1806 and imposed German-sounding names on the Polish Jews, the Prussian authorities used *Geduld* in the sense of "peace," and the name is the Prussian translation of Solomon, which in other areas was often translated into Friedman or Fried.

GEFFEN (O) Geffen is the Hebrew for "vine." The name was assumed by a wine merchant. Other forms are Gaffen and Geffner.

GEIGER (O) "Violinist," in German.

GENDEL (M) Hanah becomes in Yiddish the affectionate Hene or Hendel. Since the Russian alphabet has no letter "h," it is always replaced with a "g," and among Russian Jews Hendel became Gendel.

GERSTEIN (P) A disguised version of Gershon. Another form is Gerstner.

GIBLICHMAN (O) *Giblich* is an old Yiddish word for "lilac," and the name was assumed by one who grew or sold lilacs.

GIESSER (O) Giesser or Gisser is a short form of Zinngiesser, one who made pewter ware.

GINSBURG (G) From Gunzburg, a town in Bavaria. The name was first assumed by Jews exiled from Bavaria in the sixteenth century. In 1804 many Russian Jews who had to assume family names selected the name Gunzburg in various forms, even though they were not related to the original family. The name had become popular in Russia because of the family of St. Petersburg bankers, philanthropists, and spokesmen for the Jewish community. There are records of some of the original bearers going to court to prohibit strangers from assuming the name. They did not succeed, however, and as a result thousands of families assumed the name Ginsburg.

Some Jews selected the name Gunzburg as a garbled version of Koenigsberg, formerly capital of East Prussia.

GITTELMACHER (O) Hittelmacher ("cap maker," in Yiddish) becomes among Russian Jews Gittelmacher.

GITTELMAN (S) *or* (O) Among Polish or German Jews the name means "husband of Gittel." Among Russian Jews it stands for Hittelman and means a "cap maker."

GITTELSON (M) Son of Gittel.

GLASS (O) Someone in the glass trade. Other names are Glassman and Glazer.

GLICK (M) This is the Yiddish (German, *Glück*) derived from a popular name for women in the Middle Ages, Gluckel. The name was associated with the meaning of "luck," and a number of family names were derived from it: Glick, Glickman, Glicksman, Glickstein, Glickberg, Glicksberg, Glickstern, Glickselig, Glickin. The Yiddish forms contain the element Glick and the older German forms retain the element Gluck.

GOITEIN (G) From Kojetein, a town in Moravia. Also appears in forms Gutein, Kojeteiner.

GOLDBART (D) This name means "gold beard" in German. Since Jews wore beards, their color and appearance often determined their family name. Thus we have Gelbart ("yellow beard"), Grossbart ("large beard"), Graubart ("gray beard"), Rothbart ("red beard"), Weisbart ("white beard"), Schwartzbart ("black beard"), Eisbart ("a beard that looked like white icicles").

GOLDBERG (G) *or* (M) *or* (F) Goldberg is one of the most widespread Jewish family names. There is actually a place called Goldburgh in Silesia, where the first Goldberg lived more than six hundred years ago, and this is the source of the name. When the Jews were expelled from Silesia in the fourteenth century, a number of them took Goldberg as their family name. This, however, does not explain why there are more than 60,000 Goldbergs in the United States alone; they certainly are not all descended from those few families. Actually, the name was easily adopted by many others who had no relationship to the original Silesian Jews. Many Jews honored a matriarch by the name of Golda by assuming the family name Goldberg. Other matronymics for Golda are:

Gold, Goldman, Goldner, Gilden, Goldbaum, Goldenbaum, Goldenberg, Goldblum, Goldbrunn, Goldfeder, Goldfish, Goldhaber, Goldheim, Goldhammer, Goldhirsch, Goldsand, Goldkorn, Goldkraut, Goldmark, Goldich, Goldreich, Goldschild, Goldschlag, Goldstadt, Goldstaub, Goldstern, Goldstrom, Goldenthal, Goldzweig, Goldblatt, Goldblitt, Goldfluss, Goldkrantz.

GOLDSCHEIDER (O) Literally "a separator of gold from silver." A name assumed by a goldsmith or a gold refiner.

GOLDSCHMIDT (O) *or* (P) A goldsmith. Sometimes it is a name selected by an Uri or Betzalel, since in the Bible Betzalel ben Uri was the goldsmith who fashioned the articles in the Tabernacle.

GOLDSTEIN (O) In German, the literal meaning is "touchstone," a goldsmith's tool used to test the quality of gold and silver. Many goldsmiths took the name Goldstein as a symbol of their trade.

GOLOMB (P) Golomb is the Polish for Yonah (Jonah), "dove."

GOLUB (P) The Russian version of the Czech or Ukrainian Holub, "dove," the translation of the Hebrew name Yonah (Jonah).

GOMPERTZ (P) This comes from the old German name Gundbert. Gumpert (Gompert) was frequently added to the Hebrew names Ephraim and Mordecai as early as the fourteenth century. It first appears as a family name at the end of the sixteenth century. There are a number of variants of this name such as: Gomperz, Gompers, Kompert, Kumpert, Gumpertz, Gumprecht, Gumpel, Gimpel, Gimbel.

GOODMAN (P) *or* (M) This is an English version of the Jewish name Gutman, and Gutman is the translation of the Hebrew name Tuviah. Sometimes Goodman is a matronym for Gute (which is more common as Gittel) in the following forms: Guter, Gutter, Gutterman, Gutfeld, Gutfreund, Gutreich, and Gutstein.

GORDON (F) There is no satisfactory explanation for the derivation

of the name Gordon. The name Jordan appears in central
Europe in the fifteenth century and some take Gordin,
Gordan, Gordon as variants of the Biblical river. The name
Gordon, which is widespread among non-Jews in England, is
believed to have been introduced there by a Christian order,
Gordano, which came from Italy (Gordano is the Italian
name for the river Jordan). Some believe that Jews coming
from the city and district of Grodno in Russian Poland would
ordinarily be called Grodner, but instead of assuming the
name Grodner they chose Gordon. I believe that the most
logical explanation is the following: the word for "town" in
Russian is *gorod*. *Gorodin* means "townsman" and this
became Gordin and Gordon, the last especially under English
influence.

GOTTINGER (G) From Göttingen, a town in Germany.

GOULD (M) Gould is an older form of the word "gold."

GRABER (O) Graber today means "gravedigger" in German, but an
older meaning is "engraver of seals." This was a well-
established Jewish trade in the eighteenth century. Other
German trade names of this category are: Steinschneider,
Stempel, and Stempelmacher.

GRAIVER (G) From Grajewo, a town in Poland.

GRATZ (G) From a town in the province of Posen, Germany.

GREENBERG (G) There is a town of Greenberg in Hesse, Germany,
and a Greenberg in Silesia. This latter town was formerly an
important center of wool weaving. Polish and Russian wool
would be imported and material known as "Grünberg" cloth
would be exported. Many Jews were in this business and were
known as "Grünberg merchants." When they had to take
permanent family names, many of these businessmen called
themselves Greenberg.

GREENSPAN (O) Greenspan is the German word for verdigris, a
green pigment used in dyeing and in medicine. The English
word comes from *verd de Grece*, the green of Greece. The
German word is "green of Spain," because this copper

pigment came to Germany from Spain. The name was assumed by one who sold this pigment.

GROBTUCH (D) The kind of clothes worn by an individual often determined the name given him by the authorities. Grobtuch indicates that the person named was wearing a coarse material, just as Feintuch describes the fine material of his garment.

GUGGENHEIM (G) From the village of Guggenheimb, Germany (now called Jugenheim). Other variations of the name are Guggenheimer, Guckenheim, Gougenheim.

GURLAND (G) A variation of Kurland (Courland), a Latvian province.

GUTMACHER (O) A Slavic form of *Hutmacher,* "hat maker."

HAAS (P) *Has* or *Hase* means "hare" in German, but the name has no connection with the animal. Joseph (Yosef) often had Has or Hase as a nickname, and in Yiddish the nickname was Hoos. In Dutch the word Haas means "hare" and is a Dutch-Jewish family name for the patronym Joseph.

HABER (O) At first glance Haber looks like the German-Yiddish for "oats." Actually it is the Hebrew *haber (haver),* an associate *dayan* (judge) of a rabbinic court.

HAFFKIN (M) A version of Havkin or Chavkin, "descendant of Havah."

HAHN (P) *or* (H) *or* (D) Hahn means "rooster" in German and there were two houses in Frankfurt that had the sign of the Red Rooster and the sign of the Golden Rooster. It may also be an unpleasant name conferred by the naming officials upon the bearer. Finally, Hahn became a byname for several Hebrew first names such as Hanoch, Elhanan and Manoah.

HALEVY (L) Halevy or Halevi is the Hebrew for "the Levite."

HALPERIN (G) This is one of the most widespread Jewish names. It is derived from the city of Heilbronn in Württemberg, Germany, where it was first assumed about four hundred years ago. There are many variations and some are: Heilpern, Halper, Helpern, Heilbrun, Heilbron, Heilbronner, Heilprun, Alpron, Alpern, Galpern, and Halprin.

HAMMERSTEIN (G) From Hammerstein in West Prussia.

HANDWERKER (O) Handwerker is the German for "tradesman," "artisan," such as baker, tailor, shoemaker. Another from of the name is Handwerger.

HARRIS (P) Harris is an English name and means "son of Harry (Henry)." Jews with the name Herz, Hirsh, or Aaron (nick-named Haare or Horre in Yiddish) often adopted this name in English-speaking countries.

HART/HARTMAN (P) Hart is an English name that refers to a "stag" or "deer" or "hart." Hartman is a German name which means "strong man." As a Jewish family name Hart and Hartman were selected as patronyms for Naphtali whose *kinnui* Herz (Harz) or Hirsh means "deer" or "hart." Other forms of this Jewish family name are Hardt, Hartog, Hartwig, Hartwick, Hartig.

HASPEL (O) This is a German word for the reel on which yarn is wound. The name denotes either a dealer in yarn or a seller of the reels.

HEFTER (O) A worker with gold braid and lacing, much in demand for the fashions of the seventeenth and eighteenth centuries. Jews were very involved in this trade.

HEIFETZ (P) Heifetz is a family name derived from Hefetz which means "desire," "delight." It was formerly a popular first name among eastern Jews. Another form of the name is Keyfetz.

HEIMAN, HEIMANN, HEYMAN (P) The first four letters of these names indicate the name Hayyim.

HELFGOTT (P) The German translation of Azriel ("God's help").

HELLER (G) From Halle, a town in Germany. The Russian form is Geller.

HELLMAN (P) Hellman is a form of the name Samuel. Samuel is called in the Bible *hanavi* ("the prophet"), and his name was translated into German Helman ("clairvoyant," "prophet"). It appears in the forms Hillman, Elman, Ellman. Since Russian Jews substitute a "g" for an "h," the eastern European version of the name is Gellman, Gilman.

HERSHDORFER (P) Hershdorfer is an extension of the name Hersch or Hirsch ("hart") which is a *kinnui* of the Hebrew Naphtali. Other forms of the patronyms for Hirsch are Hirschbruk, Hirschburg, Hirschfeld, Herschfus, Hirschwald, Hirschthal, Hirschman, Hirschberg, Hirschbaum, Hirschhaut, Hirschkopf, Hirschler, Hirschkorn, Hershson, Hershstein, Herstein.

HERZ (P) The *kinnui* of Naphtali is Herz ("hart"), or Hersch. From this we also get such names as Hertz, Hertzman, Hertzmark, Hirschman, Gershman, Gersh, Gertz, Gershovitz, and Herskowitz.

HEUER, HAUER (O) A butcher.

HILDESHEIM (G) From Hildesheim, a town in Hannover, Germany.

HINDIN (M) *Hinde* is the German for a female deer, and the Jewish first name Hinde or Hinda is often associated with this meaning. It is possible, however, that the name Hinde is one version of Hanah (via Hendl, Henda). Hindin would then mean "descendant of Hannah." Other forms of the name are Hindes, Hindus, Indis, Indes.

HIRSCHHORN (G) *or* (H) *or* (P) It may be derived from a town in Germany or from the sign of house No. 103 in Frankfurt or an extended form of the name Hersch ("hart"), the *kinnui* for Naphtali.

HIRZHMAN (O) *Hirzh* is Yiddish for millet; the name denotes a dealer in millet.

HODES (M) Hadassah, the Hebrew name for Esther, popularly

became Hodi, Hodel, Hode, Hudel. Hodes means "descendant of Hode (Hadassah)."

HOFFMAN (O) *or* (F) The German word *Hofman* is a farmer who owns his land. Possibly, a Jew taking this name was such a farmer. Other Jews selected the name Hoffman from their employment at the court *(Hof)* of a prince or duke. Most Jewish Hoffmans selected the name as a symbol of Hoffnung ("hope") and Hoffman meant "a man of hope."

HOLZMAN (O) Jews were engaged in the wood and lumber trade in the timber areas of Europe. Holz is the German for "wood" or "timber" and Holzman (Holtzman), Holz (Holtz), Holzer (Holtzer), and the Slavic equivalents Goltzer, Goltz, Goltzman are the names commonly associated with the timber trade.

HOROWITZ (G) Horowitz and all of its many variations in spelling is taken from the Bohemian town of Horovice, where the first Horowitz family originated in the fifteenth century. Horwitz, Gorwitz, Gurvich, and Urevich are common variants. As in the case of all famous family names, Horowitz was adopted by many Jews who had no relationship to the original branches.

HUBERMAN (O) *Huber* is Yiddish for "oats" and Huberman is an oat dealer. Among Russian Jews, the name becomes Guberman.

IMBER (O) Imber is Polish for "ginger." In Yiddish the word is *ingber*. This name was assumed by a groceryman who sold this item.

ITKIN (M) The name Yetta or Yitta may be derived from Henrietta or from Yudis (the nickname originally being Yutka). Yitta plus the Russian patronymic suffix *-kin* gives us Yitkin or Itkin.

JAFFE (P) *or* (M) The name Kalonymos ("beautiful name") is a Greek version of the Hebrew Shem Tov and was popular among the Jews in the Middle Ages. In the sixteenth century one family selected only the translation of Kalon ("beautiful") as the family name in the Hebrew form of Jaffe *(Yafeh)*. Later on, other Jews selected the name in tribute to a matriarch by the name of Shayndel (from the Yiddish which means "beautiful"). The name also appears as Yaffe, Yaffin, and Joffin, Jaffin.

JASTROW (G) From Jastrow, a city in Prussia.

KABAKOFF (O) In Russian, it means "tavern keeper." In Ukrainian, it means a dealer in pumpkins.

KADAR (O) Kadar is Hungarian for "cooper."

KADURY (G) A very distinguished Jewish family from Baghdad bears the name Kadury or Kadoorie. In former generations this family had business and residential ties with the Malabar coast of southwest India, especially in the province of Kadur. This area of India has had a Jewish population since the first Christian century.

KAFKA (H) *or* (O) *or* (P) Kafka or Kavka is Czech for "crow" and may indicate a person who lived in or near a house with the sign of this bird. In Polish, Kawka is a dealer in coffee. Some have derived Kafka as a nickname from Yaakov (Jacob). Yaakov becomes Koppel, which becomes Kopke, and this in turn is transformed to Kapke and Kafka.

KAGANOFF (L) Kahn, a form of *kohen* becomes Kagan among Russian Jews. The suffix *-off* indicates descent, and Kaganoff means "descended from a *kohen.*"

KALUZNA (G) From Kaluszyn, a town in Poland.

KARELITZ (G) Yiddish form of Korelicze, a town in White Russia.

KARLIN (G) A surburb of Pinsk, Poland. Other forms of the name are Karlinsky and Karliner.

KARTAGENER (O) There was a certain kind of beans that were called kartaginian beans because they supposedly originated in ancient Carthage. Kartagener was a name assumed by a dealer of these beans.

KATZ (A) *and* (L) Katz has nothing to do with cats but is an acronym for k*ohen* tz*edek*, "priest of righteousness." It is based on Psalm 132:9 which says "Your priests will be clothed in righteousness." Kohen Tzedek appears as the name of the Gaon of Pumbedita in the tenth century. As a family name, it first appears in the seventeenth century.

KATZOFF (O) A rendition of the Hebrew word for "butcher." Other forms are Katziff, Kaciff, Kacev.

KAUFMAN/KAUFMANN (P) *or* (O) The name in German means "merchant" or "shopkeeper" and a few Kaufmans probably were merchants. As a Jewish name Kaufman is derived from Jacob (Yaakov) which becomes Yakovman, then Yakofman, then is shortened to Kofman and emerges as Kaufman.

KAVINOKY (D) This name is based on a Talmudic expression *kav venaki*, which means "only a *kab* (a small quantity) but *naki* ('pure')." This name was given as tribute to a person small in size but with many qualities of character.

KAZAN (O) A form of the Hebrew word *hazan*, "cantor."

KELMAN (P) As a non-Jewish name Kelman is a name assumed by a bricklayer, one who works with a trowel *(Kelle*, in German). As a Jewish name, Kellman is another version of Kalman, which is a short form of Kalonymos, the Greek translation of Shem Tov ("good name").

KEMMELMAN (O) A seller of combs and other notions. *Kemml* is "comb" in Yiddish.

KEMPLER (G) From Kemblow, a town in Galicia.

KIMMELMAN (O) A seller of caraway and other spices; a retail grocer or food merchant. *Kimmel* is "caraway." Spices provide a number of family names to indicate one involved in merchandising them: Gewirtz, Gewirtzman *(gewirtz* is Yiddish for "spice"), Fenichel (from *Fenchel*, "fennel," in German), Muskat (the leaf of nutmeg), Zimring, Zimmet, Zinneman ("cinnamon"), Pepper and Feffer, Nelken ("cloves").

KIRMEYER (O) From the German *Kirchmeier*, "the operator of a church farm." As a Jewish family name it indicates an official in the synagogue *(gabbai)*.

KIRSTEIN, KIRSTEN (P) As a Gentile name, it is derived from an ancestor whose name was Christian. As a Jewish name it is a veiled form for the name Gershon or Gershom. The disguise of the name was further developed in the form Kirsche, and a variety of combinations were created: Kirchstein, Kirchen, Kirschheim, Kirschdorf, Kirschenberg, Kirschenzweig, Kirschenblatt, and Kirschenbaum.

KIRZNER (O) A furrier (from Yiddish).

KISCH (G) From Chiesch, a town near Eger, Bohemia.

KISSELEVICH (G) From Kisielowka, a village in the Ukraine.

KISSINGER (G) From Kissingen, a town in Bavaria, Germany.

KITAY (G) An abbreviated form of Kitaygorod (the town of the Chinese), a small town in Podole, Russia.

KIVEL (G) *or* (P) Either from Kiwile, the name of several villages in Lithuania, or a nickname for Akiva.

KLASS (A) *and* (O) Klass is the acronym k*le zemer,* the musical ensemble that entertained at weddings, etc. The group was commonly called the *Klezmer.*

KLEBAN (G) From Kleban or Klebanie, a village in the Ukraine.

KLEPFISH (O) A Yiddish version of Klippfisch ("stockfish"), cod or haddock, salted or dried. The bearer of this name was a merchant of this commodity.

KLINGER (O) As a Jewish name it indicates a junk dealer, from *Klunker* ("junk," in German)

KOBRIN (G) From Kobryn, a town in the district of Grodno, Russia. The name appears also in the form Kobriner.

KOENIG (P) *or* (D) Koenig is the German for "king" and is often a translation of the Hebrew name Melekh (king) or Elimelekh (God is King). Sometimes a person who played the part of the king in the Purim *shpil* (the special dramatic presentations of

the festival of Purim) would be dubbed Koenig and this name
became his family name. Finally, some of the naming officials
would make sport of some poor or wretched Jew by giving
him the name "king."

KOENIGSBERG (G) The capital of East Prussia.

KOHUT (P) *or* (H) *or* (D) Kohut is Ukrainian for "rooster." It is
either a translation of the name Hahn, which means "rooster"
in German, or a reference to the house sign of the red rooster
or the golden rooster in Frankfurt, or it may be an unpleasant
name conferred by the naming officials upon the bearer.

KOLATCH (O) Kolatch or Kolitz is a reference to *Kolatch*, the
Yiddish among Russian-Polish Jews for holiday and Sabbath
white bread. The name was taken by a baker.

KOLODKIN (G) From Kolodky, a town in Lithuania.

KOLODNY (G) *or* (O) Either from Kolodno, a town in what was
formerly Poland, or a cooper, because Kolodno derives from
the word meaning log and was a lumber center.

KONOTOPSKY (G) From Konotop, a town in the district of
Chernigov, Russia.

KOPELOVICH (P) Yaakov (Jacob) became Yaakobel, which became
Kobel or Kopel. Kopelovich and Kopeloff mean "son of
Yaakov." The English equivalent would be Jacobson.

KORENTAYER (O) The Yiddish for "grain appraiser."

KORF, KORFF (O) From the German *Korf* ("basket"). A basket
maker.

KORN (O) *or* (L) Korn is the German word for "grain" and this may
indicate a grain dealer. But many of the Jewish family names
that contain the element Korn (or Corn) are really disguised
forms for Kohen (Cohen). See Cornfeld.

KORSHAK (H) *or* (O) Either from the Ukrainian word "eagle,"
which would make the name an equivalent of Adler, or from
Korczak, which in Polish is "wine glass." This may indicate a

sign on a tavern or roadside inn and the name was assumed by its owner.

KOSHES (F) From the Hebrew *keshet*, the zodiac sign of Saggitarius. The zodiac sign is called in Hebrew *mazal*, which is the word "luck." The bearer assumed this name perhaps during the time of the year under which this sign was, with the additional idea that it bring him good luck.

KOSLOWSKY (G) From Koslowsk, a town in Lithuania. Also appears as Kaslowsky.

KOSSOWSKY (G) From Kossow, a town in Poland or Kossov, in Russia.

KOTELSCHIK (O) "Kettlemaker," "boilermaker," in Russian.

KOTLAR (O) The Yiddish form of the Polish *Kotlarz*, a maker of pans or other kitchenware out of copper.

KOVARSKY (G) *or* (O) If it is from Polish or Lithuanian, it indicates the town of Kowarsk, in Lithuania. If it is from a region in Czechoslovakia, it may indicate the occupation of smith or worker in metals.

KOZIN (G) From Kozin, a town in Volhynia, Russia.

KRAINES, KRAININ (M) Kreindel is a medieval Yiddish feminine name adopted from the German *Krone* ("crown"). It was further changed into Kreine. Kreinin is the Slavic matronym and Kreines is the German form. The meaning is "descendant of Kreine."

KRASNY (M) The Russian for "red" or "beautiful." As a family name it is a translation of Hanah, or Bayla, or Shayndel.

KRATCHMER (O) Kratchmer is the Yiddish for the operator of a *kretchme* ("country inn"). Inns were practically a Jewish monopoly in Poland. The name sometimes appears as Kretchmer or Krachman.

KRAUS (D) Kraus in German means "curly." Kraus, Krauss, and Krause describe a curly-headed person. So do the family names Kraushaar ("curly hair") and Krauskopf ("curly head").

KRENSKY (O) This family name is derived from Kremski, the name of a bleach used for textiles throughout Russia and Poland. It was originally invented in the Austrian town of Krems and was called Kremsierweiss ("Krems white"). The name was assumed by one who sold this item.

KRETSKES (M) The male name Zemach ("branch," in Hebrew) became Crescas among Spanish Jews and a feminine form of the name was Cresca. Among Polish Jews this name was "improved upon" and transformed into Kretske. Kretskes means "one descended from Kretske."

KRICHEVSKY (G) From Krichev, a town in the district of Mohilev, Russia.

KRIPKE (G) The Yiddish version of the town of Krupka in White Russia.

KRISCHER (G) The Hungarian town of Szent-Kereszt (Holy Cross) is called in Slavic Svaty Krish. In Yiddish it was shortened to Krish. Krisher means "one coming from Krish."

KROCHMAL (O) Krochmal in Yiddish is "starch," and the name indicates a manufacturer or a dealer in starch. Another form of the name is Krochmalnik.

KRONISH (P) In the early Middle Ages, Jews in Poland often bore pure Slavic first names. Kronish is an old Slavic personal name Chronislav ("glory of the times"). Later, when personal names became family names, this name also was adopted and modified to the shorter form.

KRULEWITZ (G) From Krolewiec, a town near Kiev in the Ukraine.

KRUMBEIN (D) Literally, "crooked-legged" or "bow-legged" person.

KRUPNICK (O) A manufacturer of groats, popularly known among Jews as *kasha*.

KULEFSKY (G) From the village of Kolowo in Lithuania. Sometimes appears as Kolowski.

KULIKOWSKY (G) From Kulikow, a town in Galicia. Also appears as Kulik.

KUPIETZ (O) "Merchant," in Ukrainian.

KUPPENHEIM (G) From Kuppenheim, a town in Baden, Germany. Sometimes appears as Kippenheim.

KUSHNER (O) In Polish *kusnierz* is a furrier and in Ukrainian *kushnir* denotes a furrier. Kushner is the Yiddish form. Jews were involved in the furrier trade for many years. In eastern Europe the furriers catered mostly to men who wore expensive fur-trimmed garments and headgear. Kurschner and Futterman have the same meaning and origin.

KUTNER (G) From Kutno, a town in Poland.

KUTOFF (G) Kutoff or Kutower is derived from Kuty in Polish Galicia.

KWILECKI (G) From Kwilcz, a village in Prussian Poland.

LACHMAN (P) *or* (G) The name is usually taken as a German translation of Isaac ("he laughed"). Others derive Lachman from *Lache,* the old German for "boundary mark" and the name would mean the man who lived at the boundary. The most recent view among scholars is that Lachman was the way non-Jews in Silesia pronounced Nahman. The name appears as early as the fifteenth century as a first name and later was adopted as a family name.

LADANY (G) From Ladany in Hungary.

LAFFER (O) The Yiddish form of Laufer, a traveling furrier. The name often appears as Leiffer.

LAGOVER (G) From Lagow, a town in Poland.

LAKIN (M) Leah is often nicknamed Layke. Lakin is a descendant of Leah.

LANDAU (G) From Landau, a town in Bavaria. When the city expelled its Jews in 1545, the refugees moved to Prague. Here the name first appears.

LANDMAN/LANDMANN (D) Literally, "man from the province." But as a Jewish name it is often a garbled version of the Hebrew *lamdan*, "scholar."

LANGSAM (D) Langsam is a German word for "slow," "easy-going." The name was conferred by the state officials because the person given the name was slow.

LAPIDUS (P) *or* (O) Lapidus is a Biblical name and became a family patronymic. Others interpret Lapidus as Latin *lapides*, a translation of Steiner ("stones," in German). According to this latter interpretation the name would indicate the occupation of a stone mason or a gem engraver.

LAPIN (G) There are a number of Polish and Russian communities called Lapin or, in Yiddish, Lapine. The name appears in both forms.

LASKOV (G) From Laskowicze, a town in White Russia, formerly Lithuania, or from Laskowicze in Galicia. The name appears also as Laskowitz.

LAUTENBERG (G) From Lautenberg, a town in West Prussia.

LAWENTMAN (O) From the Yiddish for "linen" (*lavent*). The name would indicate a weaver or dealer in linen.

LEBOWITZ (P) A variant of Leibowitz.

LEDERER (O) Lederer is "tanner," in German. The name appears also as Lederman. Farber is also a name associated with the dyeing of leather.

LEFF (P) Polish for "lion," which is the translation of the Yiddish Layb, the *kinnui* of Judah. It also appears as Lew and Liff.

LEHMAN/LEHMANN (O) *or* (L) Lehman (n) is a technical term from the Middle Ages and means a vassal of a feudal lord. As a Jewish family name it is derived from the profession of banking or money lending. In German *leihen* means "to lend," and *Leihhaus* is a pawnshop and *Leihman* was the pawnbroker. This became Lehman(n). The name may also be a disguised name for a Levite. Lehman was understood as Levi-man.

LEIBOWITZ (P) The Yiddish *kinnui* of Judah is Layb (Leib), plus -*owitz*, the Slavic suffix meaning "son of."

LEKACH (O) Lekach is Yiddish for "honeycake." The name was assumed by a baker. Another form of the name is Lekachman.

LEMPERT (F) Lempert means "leopard," and this name is a reference to Pirke Avot 5:23, which states: "Be bold as a leopard to do the will of your Father in Heaven." The name appears also as Lemport and Lampert.

LENOFF (G) From Leniew, a village in Poland.

LEPAVSKY (G) From Libau or Libava, a town in Latvia.

LERNER (O) Lerner means "student" in Yiddish or German. In eastern Europe a young husband devoted all of his days to study Torah, while his wife or other members of the family took care of making a living.

LEVANDULA (O) "Lavender," in Hungarian. From the lavender shrub came an oil used in making perfume and soap. The bearer of this name was in the cosmetic trade.

LICHT (P) A name selected for Uri or Meir because of its association with "light." Jewish family names beginning with Licht, ("light, in German) are usually a reference to this patronymic: Lichtenstein, Lichtenberg, Lichtenfeld.

LICHTERMAN (O) In the eighteenth century the Russian and Austrian governments imposed a special tax on the candles used by Jews for the Sabbath. The collection of this tax was farmed out to certain individuals, who were called in Yiddish or German, Lichterman ("candleman") or Pechter.

LICHTZER (O) Derived from *Lichtzieher* ("candle dipper," in German). This name is the equivalent to the English name Chandler.

LIEBERMAN (P) This name is a curious development from Eliezer. Eliezer became Eliezerman, which was abbreviated to Lieserman. Lieserman ultimately became Lieberman.

LIFSHITZ (G) From Loebschutz, a town in Upper Silesia, or

Liebeschitz, in Bohemia, there developed a variety of Jewish family names: Lifschitz, Lipschitz, Libschitz, Lipschuetz, Luepschuetz.

LIGORNER (O) From the Polish *lugarniarz,* a bleacher of cotton cloth.

LINETSKY (G) From Linets, a town in the Ukraine.

LINKER (D) Linker may describe one who is left-handed, gawky, or gangling.

LIPMAN (P) Lipman is a *kinnui* of Eliezer. Eliezer was often associated with the German name Gottlieb. Gottlieb was shortened to Lieb, which was in turn lengthened to Liebman or Lipman. Lipman appears as Lipa or Lapman. Variations of this name are Lipkin and Litman. Lipis or Lipes is another patronymic form.

LIPSKY (G) The word *lipa* is Slavic for "linden tree" and is the source of many place names. The most famous of these is the city of Leipzig, in Germany, which was originally called Lipsk because of its many linden trees. Leipzig, or Lipsk, was famous because of the great fairs that were annually held there and which were attended by Jewish merchants. Lipsky means "one who traveled to Lipsk or Leipzig."

LITWACK (G) *Litwa* is Lithuania in Russian and Polish, as is *Lite* in Yiddish. This has given us the names Litwack, Littauer, Litwin, Litvak, Littman, Litant, all of which mean "a Jew from Lithuania."

LOME (G) From Lomi, a town in Lithuania.

LOPATA (O) "Shovel" or "oar," in Polish. It is a name often used by a baker. Other forms are Lopatnik and Lopatnikov.

LORSCH (G) From Lorge, a town in Hesse, Germany. Other forms are Lorge and Lorig.

LOTSTEIN (O) From the German *Loetstein,* "soldering stone." The name was taken by a glazier who used solder in his work.

LOWENSTEIN (P) *or* (L) *Löwe* means "lion" in German and may be a translation of the Yiddish Layb which is the *kinnui* or byname for Judah (Yehudah). Löwe may also be a disguised form for Levi, signifying Levitic descent. The *-stein* is an embellishment.

LOWITZ (G) From Lowicz, a town in Poland.

LUBAN (G) From Luban, a town in the province of Minsk, Russia.

LUBAR (G) From Lubar, a town in the Ukraine. Other forms of the name are Luber and Lubarsky.

LUBIN (G) From Lubin, a town in Poland.

LUBOWITZ (G) From Lubowicz, a town in Poland.

LUKATZKY (G) From Lukatz, or Lokatz, a town in Poland. Another form of the name is Lukacher.

LUNZ (G) From Louans, a town in France. In Hebrew it became Loantz which was rendered in Polish as Lunz.

LURIA (G) One tradition traces the name from Luria, a town in the province of Treviso, Italy. Due to religious persecution the Jews of Luria left Italy for Germany and thence to Poland, Lithuania, and Russia. Another tradition traces the name to Loria, a town near Bassano, Italy. The name first appears in Alsace in the fifteenth century. Luria appears in the forms Lurje and Lurie.

LUSTIG (P) A name, meaning "joyful" in German, often selected as a translation of the Hebrew Simhah.

LUZZATTO (G) The name of a distinguished Italian family. It goes back to the sixteenth century when the first members of the family came to Italy from the German province of Lausitz, which was called Lusatia and became in Italian Luzzatto. Some members of the family called themselves Luzzatti.

LYSAGORA (G) This is from the Polish word for "bald mountain," to describe a treeless mountaintop. There are a number of places throughout Poland which bear this name. The name is often anglicized to Lisagor.

MAGIDSON (P) *and* (O) Son of the preacher *(maggid*, in Hebrew). Another form is Magida. Magid sometimes appears as Magit.

MAGTAZ (A) *and* (P) Magtaz stands for m*igeza* t*ure zahav*, from the family of *Ture Zahav*, a book authored by Rabbi David ben Samuel Halevi who, because of his work, is called the TAZ.

MAHLER (O) One who grinds grain, "miller," in German.

MAITES (M) Descended from *Maite* ("maiden," in old German; the English equivalent is Virginia). Another form of the name is Maitin, Meitin, Meites.

MALECH (G) From Malech, a town in White Russia.

MALEV (G) Malev or Malevsky from Malewo, the name of a number of places throughout Poland and Russia.

MALIN (G) From Malin, a town near Kiev in the Ukraine.

MALKES (M) From Malkah, a woman's name, meaning "queen" in Hebrew (the reference is to the Biblical Esther). Other forms are Malkov, Malkoff, Malkin, Malkinson.

MANEWITZ (G) Yiddish form of the Russian village Maniowce. It has been anglicized to Manewith.

MANISCHEWITZ (P) Manisch is either a short form of Menahem or of Menashe, and Manischewitz means "son of Manisch."

MANISHEN (G) The Yiddish version of Maniusin, a town in Poland.

MANKOVSKY (G) From Mankowce, the name of a number of localities in Poland, Lithuania, and the Ukraine.

MANKUTA (D) From the Polish *mankut*, "left-handed."

MANNHEIM (G) A city in Baden, Germany.

MAPU (A) The family name of Abraham Mapu, who first introduced the novel into Hebrew literature. He fashioned the name out of his own first name, the names of his grandfathers, and the town the family came from. The name is an acronym of *M*oshe, *A*braham, *P*inhas, and the town Vasilishok.

MARAM (P) *and* (A) Maram, or Marum, was originally the *kinnui* of

Meir and was an acronym for M*orenu* H*arav* M*eir*, in honor of Rabbi Meir of Rothenburg, the greatest Jewish scholar in Germany in the thirteenth century. Members of families who traced their descent from him and many of his disciples named their sons in his honor. This name has continued for more than seven centuries, first as a personal name and later, when family names were adopted, as a family name. Beginning in South and West Germany, the name was carried among families into Bohemia and Moravia and followed the movement of German Jews into other places.

MARANS (O) Marans is a form of Marantz, which is an abbreviation of *Pomerantz,* "orange," in Yiddish and German. This fruit was a great delicacy in Europe and a dealer in it was held in special regard.

MAREMONT (G) From Marymont, a village near Warsaw, built by Queen Marie Sobieska.

MARGOLIN (M) *Margola* is the Hebrew for "pearl" and Margolin means "descendant of Pearl."

MARGOLIS (M) Margolis means "pearl" and is derived from the Hebrew *margalit.* It appears as early as the end of the fifteenth century as a tribute to a woman called Pearl. Other forms of the name are Margolioth, Marguiles, Margolouth.

MARKS (P) Marcus is an ancient Roman name and means "belonging to the god Mars." It has continued as a name to this day as Marcus, as Mark in English, and as Marco in Italian and Spanish. Jews with a Hebrew name of Moshe or Mordecai often selected Marcus or Mark as the non-Hebrew name. This became the family name Marks or Marx.

MARMELSTEIN (O) Yiddish for "marblestone" and may refer to one engaged in building. Or it may be a form of the Polish word *marmurek,* "grindstone," and may refer to one in this trade.

MASHBIR (O) Joseph in the Bible is called *hamashbir,* "the provider." This name was assumed by one who was a grain merchant, relating it to Joseph.

MASHBITZ (O) This is a Hebrew word and refers to a weaver of brocade or a setter of jewels.

MASS (A) *and* (O) From the Hebrew m*oker seforim,* "bookseller."

MATANKY (D) *Matanka* is a Russian and Polish word which describes the bow worn on overcoats and fur garments in place of buttons. Either the one who assumed the name or the naming officials used this item as a reference.

MATTIS (P) Mattis is a short form of the Hebrew name Mattityahu (Mattathias, Matthew). Other forms of the patronym are Mattison and Mattisoff.

MAUTNER (O) Mautner is a collector of duty or tolls.

MAZUR (G) Mazur means a native of the province of Mazowsze in central Poland. Jews coming from this area to new settlement in the Ukraine or other parts of Russia were referred to as Mazur; they later took this as their family name to indicate their place of origin.

MECKLER (O) Yiddish for "broker" or "middleman" (German *Makler*).

MEERSAND (P) *and* (F) This means "sand of the sea" and is a reference to Genesis 32:13 where Jacob is told that his descendants would number as the sands of the sea. The name was assumed by a man called Jacob or by a son of Jacob.

MEHLER (O) Mehler, or Meiler, is a charcoal burner.

MEHLMAN (O) A flour merchant.

MEISEL (P) There are two developments of this name. One is from Mordecai. Meisel, or Maizel, is an affectionate diminutive of Mordecai and goes back to the middle of the sixteenth century. A descendant of one of the early families bearing this name founded the famous Meisel's Synagogue in Prague. This name also appears in the form Meislish or Maizlish. A second development of this name is from Moshe (Moses). One form of the diminutive of Moshe is Meisel. Popularly, this was often associated with the Yiddish for "mouse," but it has nothing to do with the rodent. Nevertheless, in the Prague cemetery, on a tombstone of a women who died in 1614 and whose family name was Meisel, a mouse is inscribed on the stone.

MELBER (O) From the old German for "flour dealer."

MELEZIN (G) The Yiddish version of the town of Molozyn in White Russia.

MELLITZ (G) From Mielec, a town in Poland.

MELNICK (G) *or* (O) From the town of Mielnik, at one time part of Poland and at another time part of Lithuania. Or from Melnik, the Russian word for "miller," from which we also get Melnikoff.

MELTZ (O) *and* (F) From the Polish *mielcarz*, the owner of a malt kiln. This can also be the name for a brewer. From this we get another form, Meltzer. However, a name assumed by Rabbi Isser Zalman Meltzer had nothing to do with this occupation but was based on the Hebrew word *meltzer* ("steward") in Daniel 1:16.

MELZNER (O) Melzner, or Meltsner, is a dealer in malt and designates a brewer or malter.

MENBA (A) This is a reference to an ancestor who had died and about whom the Hebrew phrase m*enuhoto* b*eden* ("may his rest be in the Garden of Eden") was used. Another form of the name is Manba.

MENDEL (P) Mendel is the *kinnui* for Menahem which means "comforter" in Hebrew. It is one of the names for the Messiah and a name that was given to boys born during the week after Tisha B'Av. The name was elaborated in many ways and appears in a variety of forms: Mandel, Mendheim, Mendthal, Mendelheim, Mendelberg, Mendelsberg, Mandelstamm, Mandelbaum, Mandelbrodt, Mandelblum, Mandelsuss, Mandelman, Menkin.

MENUCHIN (M) Since the Middle Ages Menuhah ("tranquility") is a Hebrew name for a woman. Menuchin or Menuhin means "son of Menuhah."

MERR (P) Merr, or Meer, is a form of Meir.

MESLIN (G) Meslin, or Maslin, is from the village of Meslany in Lithuania. The name also appears as Meslansky.

MESSINGER (O) *Messing* is German for "brass." A dealer or worker in brass.

METCHIK (G) From Mieczyk, a town in Poland.

MEYEROFF (P) In German *Meyerhoff* is "the owner of a dairy farm," but Jewish names in combination with Meyer are almost always an elaborated form of Meir (meaning "light," in Hebrew). Thus, we have the following: Meyerfeld, Meyerheim, Meyersberg, Meyerstein, Meyerhardt, Meyersicht, Meyers.

MIHÁLY (G) From Mihály, a town in Hungary.

MILGROM (F) The pomegranate was considered a symbol of life and fertility. In Yiddish this fruit is called *milgrom.*

MILHAUD (G) Milhaud is a village in France. It is a common Jewish name in southern France.

MILLER (O) The Yiddish for "miller."

MILLMAN (O) A miller.

MILSTEIN (O) "Millstone," in German. A name assumed by a miller.

MINKOVSKY (G) From Minkowce, a town in the district of Podolia, Russia.

MINOWITZ (G) From the village of Miniowitz, or Maniowitz, in Volynia, Russia.

MINTZ (G) From the German city of Mainz. Other forms are Minc, Menz, or Munz.

MIRMAN (G) Mirman, or Merman, denotes a native of Mergentheim, Germany.

MIRSKY (G) From Mir, a town in the province of Minsk.

MIRVIS (G) From Mierzwica, a town called in Yiddish Mervitz, or Mervis. There are many places with this name all over Russia and Lithuania.

MISHKIN (M) Mishke is an affectionate form for Miriam. Mishkin means descended from Miriam.

MLOTOK (O) *or* (P) Mlotok, or Molotok, means "little hammer." It was a name taken by a carpenter or is a translation of *Hammer,* which means "hammer" in German or Yiddish, and was used as a nickname for Hayyim.

MOGILNER (G) From Mogilno, a town in Posen.

MONSKY (P) Menahem becomes Mendel, or Mandel, and is shortened to Mann. Mannsky or Monsky means "descended from Menahem."

MONTAGU (F) Montagu is the family name of Shakespeare's Romeo and in French it means "peaked mountain." There is in England a famous Jewish family by the name of Montagu. Moses Samuel was given the name Montagu as his non-Hebrew first name and became Montagu Samuel. He later reversed his names to become Samuel Montagu, and this has remained the family name for the past one hundred fifty years.

MONTALBAN (G) A city in Aragon with a Jewish community going back to the fourteenth century. There is also a city by that name in Castille.

MORENU (O) Morenu means "our master" in Hebrew and is a title of honor for a rabbi.

MORGENSTERN (F) "Morning star," in German. It may have been a name invented by the person adopting it or by the authorities giving it. Or it may have been given to an "early bird" who came to have his name registered and was dubbed "morning star," the first to appear.

MORPURGO (G) An Italian family name originating in Marburg, Austria. Other forms of the name are Marpurg, Marpurch, Marhuc.

MOSAK (G) Mosak, or Mozak, is derived from Mossaki, a town in Poland.

MOSKOWITZ (P) *or* (G) Moskowitz may signify one who came from Moscow. But the name Moskovsky is the more common designation for geographical origin. Moskowitz usually means "descendant of Mosko," which is a Polish nickname for Moses.

MOTEFF (P) Mote is a common diminutive for Mordecai. Moteff or Motew is the Russian form meaning "son of Mordecai."

MUCHNIK (O) From the Russian word for "flour merchant."

MUNVES (P) Munves is a name that goes back to the first Christian century. King Monobaz converted to Judaism and built a magnificent palace in Jerusalem. During a year of famine he supported countless poor at his own expense and the Talmud pays great tribute to him. The rabbis mention that Jewish boys were given his name in appreciation for his great deeds. The name thus entered Judaism and later became a family name.

MYTOSKY (G) Mytosky, Mytofsky, or Mytowski is from Myto, a town in Lithuania.

NACHMAN (P) In areas where Hebrew names were forbidden, a name like Nachman assumed German forms such as Trostman, Treistman, Treister, which indicate the idea of consolation in German as does the original name in Hebrew.

NAFTULIN (P) Naftulin, Naftulis, Naftalin, are all patronyms of Naphtali.

NAGER (O) Nager, Neiger, Nuger are all from the Hebrew *nagar*, "carpenter."

NAIMAN (A) *or* (O) *or* (D) It is either derived from *shaliah neeman*, the accredited agent or the notary of a Jewish community in eastern Europe. It means trustworthy and may refer to the office of *mashgiah*, the supervisor of religious matters in the community. Or it may be a form of Neuman, a newcomer or immigrant. Or it may symbolize that the man has a new name now and is a new man.

NAPARSTEK (O) Derived from the Polish word for "thimble" and was assumed by a tailor. The German equivalent of this name is Fingerhut.

NASATIR (O) Many Jews kept their business books in the Hebrew language. One page was designated *natati (nasati,* in Ashkenazic pronunciation), "I gave," and another page was marked *kibalti,* "I received." From *natati* we get a name for a money lender or banker. We also get a family name Kibaltic.

NASHELKA (A) Nashelka is a Russian word meaning "stretcher," but the name is actually an acronym for *nisrefu al kiddush hashem,* "burned in martyrdom." This name was selected by a family in Russia to commemorate the martyrs in a pogrom.

NASS (A) *and* (P) Nass is the German for "wet," "moist." The name, however, is an acronym for n*ahum sofer,* Nahum the scribe.

NATHAN, NATHANSON (P) Nathan is the Biblical name of a prophet in the time of David.

NAYMARK (G) Naymark, Najmark, Newmark, Neumark are all forms of Newmarkt, the name of several towns in Poland and in Bohemia referring to a city's new market.

NERENBERG (O) Among Austrian and Galician Jews, Nerenberg was a kind of merchandise which included all kinds of notions—toys, buttons, needles, etc. A seller of such items assumed this name.

NETZKY (O) From the Ukrainian for "one who works with a kneading trough." A name assumed by a baker.

NEVIASER (G) A short form of Poneviaser, one who comes from Ponevias, in Lithuania.

NEVLER (G) From the town of Newel, in White Russia.

NIERENSTEIN (G) From Nierstein, a famous wine-producing village in the Rhineland.

NISSENBAUM (P) Nissen is the Yiddish for the month Nisan, which is also a first name. In areas where Jews were forbidden to assume Hebrew names, Nissen was extended to Nissenbaum and was accepted by the Austrian officials, to whom the name sounded like the German Nussbaum, "nut tree." Other disguises are Nissenholtz and Nissenfeld.

OBERLANDER (G) Austrian Jews who bear the name Oberlander came from South or West Germany. Hungarian Jews who bear this name are ones whose family originated in the Carpathian area.

OCHAKOFF (G) From Ochakoff, a town in Russia.

ODER (F) Oder is the Hebrew month Adar which is considered a very lucky month because it is the month of the birth of Moses and of the festival of Purim. A person born in Adar took this name. A variant form is Ader.

OFFEN (G) Offen, or Ofen, is the German name for Buda, part of the city of Budapest.

OHRINGER (G) From Ohringen, a town in Württemburg.

OKNER (G) From Okna, a town near Balta.

OKUN (G) From Okun, a town in Poland. Okun in Polish means "perch."

OLSHANSKY (G) From Olshani, a town in Lithuania.

OPPENHEIM, OPPENHEIMER (G) From Oppenheim, a town in Rhine Hesse.

ORENSTEIN (P) Oren is a disguised form for Aaron from which are derived a variety of patronyms: Orenthal, Orenstamm. Often an "h" is added and we get Horn, Hornstein, Hornthal. The "h" changes to "g" among Russian Jews and we get Goren and Gorenstein. Oren, or Oron, becomes the diminutive Ore or Orke, and with the Russian suffix -*in* or -*kin* we get Orkin, "descendant of Aaron."

ORLINSKY (G) Orlinsky, or Orlansky, is from the town of Orla.

OSINA (G) The Polish village of Osina has given us the name Osina, Osinsky, Oshinsky.

OSTERWEIL (P) Osterweil is an old German word for "Easter-time" and is a "translation" of the Hebrew name Pesah.

OSTROW (G) There are hundreds of villages and towns in Russia and Poland named Ostrow, from which the family names Ostrow and Ostrower are derived.

OZAROVSKY (G) From Ozarow, a town in Poland.

PACIFICO (P) It means "peaceful" and is a translation of Shelomo (Solomon) or Shalom among Sephardic Jews.

PACKER (O) "Wholesaler," in German, but as a family name it may come from *Packtraeger*, "peddler."

PAILET (P) Pailet is the Biblical name Pelet (1 Chronicles 2:47), which means "one who escapes." It was used symbolically of the Jewish people who had managed to survive oppression throughout history and was sometimes given to children who escaped some great danger prior to their birth. According to a number of authorities it is the source of the family name Feld and Feldman, because of a phonetic relationship (the "p" and "f" are interchangeable in Hebrew). Other variations of the name are: Feldheim, Feldstein, Feltenberg, Felsenberg, Felsen, Felsenbach, Felsenstein, Felsenthal, Feldbaum, Feldblum, Feldleit, Feldinger, and Feldhaus.

PAPERNICK (O) Papernick, Papirnyi, Papiermeister are names associated with the manufacturing or selling of paper. This was an industry in which Jews were involved in Russia.

PAPPENHEIM (G) A town in Mittelfranken, Bavaria.

PARNESS (D) *Parnas* is the Hebrew title for the president of the community.

PASTERNACK (O) This is the word for parsnip in Russian and the name was assumed by a dealer in vegetables or by one who served food.

PATINKIN (O) *Patinka* is Polish for "lady's slipper," and the name signifies a maker of shoes.

PAUKER (O) Pauker is a drummer.

PECHENIK (O) A baker.

PEIMAN (S) The feminine name Tzipporah was sometimes shortened to Peie. Peiman, or Peimann, means "Peie's husband."

PEKARSKY (G) From Pekary, the name of a number of villages throughout Poland and the Ukraine.

PELOFSKY (G) From Pilawa, a town in Poland.

PERGAMENT (O) In German *Pergament* is "parchment" and preserves the original Latin word which referred to Pergamon, an ancient city in Asia Minor, where this item originated. The name was assumed by a scribe.

PERLMUTTER (O) *or* (M) In most cases a dealer in mother of pearl assumed this name, but sometimes one whose mother's name was Pearl adopted this as a family name.

PERLOW (M) It means "descended from Perl." Other variations are Perlowsky, Perlin, Perles, Perlstein, Perlzweig, Persky.

PERVIN (D) "First-born," in Russian. Usually the Hebrew name Becher signifies a first-born but Pervin was more acceptable to the Russian authorities.

PESHKIN (M) From Peshe, Peshke—forms for Batyah, or from Pessel (the latter is from the French name Pucelle).

PEVSNER (G) Many people (most of them from White Russia) who have the name Pevsner trace the name to an original Posner (coming from Posen), but the relationship between Posner and Pevsner has not been established.

PFALZER (G) From Pfalz, the German name for the Palatinate.

PFORZHEIM (G) A town in Baden, Germany.

PIANKO (G) From the village of Pianki, in Poland.

PICK (P) Pick is an adaptation of the Bohemian and Polish *byk*, "bull." But the name has no connection with the animal; it is a reference to the *kinnui* of the Hebrew name Joseph, because in the Bible, Deuteronomy 33:17, Joseph is compared to a young bull.

PIKELNY (G) From Pikeln, in the district of Kovno, Lithuania.

PILCH (G) From Pilica, a town in Poland.

PINCHOFSKY (G) Pinchofsky, or Pinchefsky, is from Pinczow, a town in Poland.

PINCHUK (G) Originally Pinczuk, a native of Pinsk.

PINES (P) The diminutive of the Hebrew name Pinhas is often Pine, and Pines means "a descendant of Pinhas."

PINNER (G) From Pinne, a town in Posen.

PINSK, PINSKER, PINSKY (G) Pinsk is a city in the area of Minsk. The Jewish community goes back as early as 1506. Originally it was part of Lithuania, later becoming part of Poland, and later still becoming part of Russia.

PISER (G) The name is derived from the town of Peisern, in the area of Lodz, Poland. Other variations of the name are Paiser, Peiser, and Pizer.

PLISKEN (G) From Plisk, a town in Volhynia, Russia.

PLOTKIN (O) *Plotka* is Russian for a kind of whitefish. Plotke, Plotka, and Plotkin signify a dealer in fish.

PLOTNICK (O) One who works with wood; "carpenter," in Russian.

PODOLOV (G) Podolov, Podoloff, or Podolsky signifies a native of Podolia.

POLIER (O) This is the German word for a foreman on a construction crew of bricklayers, masons, or carpenters.

POLLOCK (G) Pollock indicates a native of Poland. It also appears in the forms Pollack and Polak. Jews in Switzerland who came from Poland carried the name Bollag.

POLSTER (O) Polster is the German for cushion or hassock (bolster). A Polsterer is an upholsterer.

POPPERS (G) The city of Frankfurt was abbreviated as F"F and since "f" and "p" are interchanged in Hebrew, the abbreviation was vocalized to become Popper, signifying "one coming from Frankfurt."

PORATH (P) In Genesis 49:22 Joseph is given the descriptive title Porath and thus a Joseph took this as a family name.

PORTNOY (O) "Tailor," in Russian. Other translations are the Polish and Ukranian Kravitz, the German Schneider, the Yiddish Sherman, and the Hebrew Chait, Hait, Hayt.

PORTUGAL (G) A reference to the town of Portigall, in Prussia.

POTASHNIK (O) A potash maker.

POTICHA (P) *or* (M) Poticha means "merrymaker" in Ukrainian and the name is either a translation of the Hebrew male name Simhah or of the Yiddish female name Frayda.

POTOK (G) Either a specific reference to Potok Zloty (Golden River), a town in eastern Galicia, or a reference to a number of places which have the word Potok ("river") in them.

PRENZLAU (G) A town in Brandenburg, Prussia.

PRESSER (O) Presser or Pressman is a name assumed by a tailor who also irons clothes.

PRIMACK (D) There was a tradition for a son-in-law to continue studying Torah after marriage and be fully supported and maintained by his father-in-law. This maintenance is called in Yiddish *kest,* and in Ukrainian and White Russian such a person was a Primack.

PRINZ (G) Prinz is the Hebrew form of the Italian city of Florence, which in Italian is Firenze. It derives from the Hebrew consonants for Florence, equivalent to "F-r-n-z" or "P-r-n-z."

PRITIKIN (D) Pritikin is the Russian word for "neighbor."

PROCHOWNIK (O) *and* (F) This name is associated with the legendary hero Abraham Prochownik, who was supposed to have been selected king of Poland in 842. The name means "a manufacturer of gun powder." The Germanized version is Pulvermacher, which can also mean "apothecary," in reference to medicinal powders.

PROSKAUER (G) From Proskau, a town in Upper Silesia.

PRUZANSKY (G) From Pruzany, a town in the area of Grodno, Russian Poland.

PUGATCH (D) "Owl," in Ukrainian. A nickname for a person's appearance.

RADZIK (G) From Radziki, a village in Poland.

RAKUSIN (G) From Rakuzino, a town in the district of Vitebsk, Russia. The anglicized forms are Racusen, Racusin, Racoosin.

RASKIN (M) Raske is a nickname for Rachel, and Raskin means "a descendant of Rachel."

RATHENAU (G) From Rathenow, a town in Brandenburg, Prussia.

RATNER (G) From Ratno, a town in Poland.

RAUCHWERKER (O) "Furrier," in German.

RAWITZ (G) From Rawicz, a town in Posen. Other variants are Reivitch and Rovish.

RAZUMNY (D) The Russian word for "clever," "sensible," "intelligent."

REGENSBERG (G) Regensberg, or Regensburg, in Bavaria.

REICHELSON (M) The Hebrew Rachel became in German-Yiddish Reichel, and Reichelson denotes "the son of Reichel." Other variations of the name containing Reichel are: Reich, Reiche, Reichman, Reichstein, Reichenheim, Reichenthal, Reichner, Reichenbaum.

REIFMAN (O) *Reifen* is "barrel hoop," in German, and the name could be that of a wine dealer or a cooper. Or it could be from the Hebrew *rofeh* ("physician"). *Raif* is Polish for the bit of a key and the name could be taken by a locksmith.

REINES (M) Reine is either an abbreviation of Katherine (Ka-the*rina*) or is the French translation of Malkah ("queen"). Reines means "descendant of Reine."

REISEN (G) The German form of Rydzyna, a town in Poland.

REITER (O) Russian Jews were very much involved in the lumber business. Large areas of forests would be leased and the lumber would be sent down the rivers to the ports. The one in charge of this operation was the *rayter*. Also, Ryter.

REITZES (M) Rose becomes Reysel, which becomes Reitza.

RELES (M) Rele is the affectionate form of the name Rose or Rebecca. Reles means "a descendant of Rele."

REMBA (A) Remba, or Rembo, is an acronym for a patronymic *R*abbi *M*oshe *b*en Avraham or an acronym for the Biblical phrase *r*abot *m*ahshavot *b*elev *i*sh, "many are the thoughts in the heart of man."

RIBALOW (O) "Fish dealer," in Polish.

RIBNICK (G) From the town in Latvia.

RIDKER (G) From Rudka, the name of many places in Poland.

RIMLAND (G) *or* (O) Rumelia was formerly located in European Turkey and is now in Greece and Bulgaria. It was a district known for its horses. The name was taken by one who came from this area or by a Jew living in Poland who imported Rumelian horses.

RINGLE (O) Ringle, Ringel, or Goldring is a name taken by a goldsmith, whose specialty was making wedding rings.

RIVKIND (M) Rivkind or Rifkind is from the name Rivke, the Yiddish for Rebecca. The ending was originally the Russian *-in* which denotes descent, but extended to *-ind*.

ROBACK (O) Roback, or Rabak, is Ukrainian for "laborer."

ROCKOFF (G) From Rakow, a town near Minsk. Other forms are: Rackover, Rakowsky, Rackofsky.

RÖDELHEIM (G) A town near Frankfurt am Main in Germany.

ROGOV (G) From Rogovo, near Kovno, Lithuania. Other forms are Rogow, Rogoff, Rogovsky, Rogover.

ROMAN, ROMANN (G) From the village of Romany (Rohmanen) in Prussia.

ROSENBERG (M) There is actually a town in western Prussia named Rosenberg but the Jewish family name is a matronymic in honor of Rosa or Rose. This name is disguised in many forms: Rosenblatt, Rosenmann ("husband of Rose"), Rosenbach, Rosenbusch, Rosenblum, Rosenblith, Rosendorf, Rosendorn, Rosenfeld, Rosengarten, Rosenhain, Rosenhaft, Rosenheim (which happens to also be a town in Bavaria), Rosenstrauch, Rosenwein, Rosenkrantz, Rosenschein, Rosenstamm, Rosenstein, Rosenstern, Rosenstock, Rosenstrauss, Rosenthal, Rosenwasser, Rosenzweig, Rosenhaus, Rosenwald, Rosenfarb, Rosenfrucht. A name like Rosenkwit is an interesting hybrid of *Rosen* (the German "rose") plus *kwit* (the Ukrainian "flower") and is a unique form of the more common Rosenblum. Roskin is "a descendant of Rose."

ROSMARIN (F) German for "rosemary," a fragrant shrub used in cookery, perfumery, and medicine all over Europe. It was formerly very popular as a flower for brides, and perhaps the name was assumed by a bridegroom in honor of his new bride.

ROSOW (G) The name of a town in the Ukraine. From it we also get the names Rossof, Rossovsky, and Rasofsky.

ROSTHOLDER (O) The anglicized version of Rosshaelter, "a keeper of horses" or "owner of a livery stable." The old German word for "horse" is *Ross*. From this we get another Jewish family name Roos, "a dealer in horses."

ROTHBERG (G) A town in Poland called in Yiddish Roytbarg, "red mountain," has given us the name Rothberg.

ROTHMAN (D) It would be name given to a redhead. Or it may be an extended form of Roth.

ROVNER (G) From Rowine, a town in Poland.

RUBEL (P) Ruvel is a diminutive of Reuven and means "little Reuven." In speech and in writing this became transformed into Rubel.

RUBENCHICK (O) *or* (P) Rubenchick *(rubenzik)* is "plane," in Polish, and the name can be taken by a carpenter or joiner. It can also mean "little Rubin," in Russian.

RUBIN (P) German for "ruby," but the name has nothing to do with a precious stone. It is derived from Reuven. Other disguises for Reuven are: Rubinstein, Rubenstein, Rubinfeld, Rubinger.

RUCHAMES (M) Ruchame is a Hebrew female name, and Ruchames, "descended from Ruchame."

RUSKIN (M) Ruska is "little Rose" and Ruskin means "descendant of Rose."

RYMER (O) Rymer is the Yiddish version of Rymarz, the Polish for "a saddler" or "harness maker."

SACHS (A) *and* (G) Sachs, Zaks, and Saks are family names that perpetuate the memory of martyrs. The acronym is *zera kodesh shemo* ("his name descends from martyrs"). A number of families trace their descent from Speyer in western Germany, which suffered much during the Crusades. Others trace the family name to martyrs in Stendal, in Prussia, where Jews were martyred in the early sixteenth century. Still others selected the name in honor of some martyr in the past without specifying the city. But these names could also mean "one coming from Saxony," and one such name appears as early as the fourteenth century. The variation would depend on the Hebrew spelling.

SAHL (A) For *Za*lman *Hale*vi or *S*ander *Hale*vi.

SALANT (G) Salant, Salanter, Salander, Sollender indicates one from Salanty, near Kovno, Lithuania.

SALINGER (P) *or* (G) Salinger, or Solinger, is either a popular variant of the Hebrew name Solomon or from Solingen, a town in Germany.

SALPETER (O) German for "saltpeter," used in fertilizer. The name indicates a seller of fertilizer.

SALZMAN (P) *or* (O) Either a disguised form for the name Solomon or a seller of salt (*Salz* is "salt," in German).

SAMETH (P) *and* (F) *or* (A) Sameth meant "velvet," but actually it is a reference to a person by the name of Shimon (Simon). The expression *siman tov* ("a lucky sign") is represented by three Hebrew letters that were used to form Sameth. Another possibility of the name is the phrase *sor mera v'ase tov*, "turn from evil and do good," which was inscribed on the lecterns of the reader's desk in synagogues of eastern Europe.

SAMTER (G) From the community of Szamotuly, in Poland.

SANDAK (D) Sandak, or Sandek, means "godfather" in the ritual of circumcision. Usually this honor was given to an outstanding individual in the family or community.

SANDITEN (G) A village in Prussia.

SAPERSTEIN (O) Made up of *sapir* ("sapphire," in Hebrew) and *Stein* ("stone," in German). The name was assumed by a jeweler.

SAPOZNIK (O) Russian for "shoemaker."

SARFATTI (G) Sarfatti, or Zarfatti, was the name of an Italian Jewish family originating in France. Tzarfat, an ancient community mentioned in the Bible, became the Hebrew word for France during the Middle Ages.

SARNA (G) From Sarna (in Poland) or Sarne (in the Ukraine). It means "place of deer."

SASPORTAS (G) A Spanish family from a place called Seisportas, "six gates."

SATANOV (G) From Satanov, a town in Podolia, Russia.

SATZ (A) or (O) Although the word *Satz* means "sentence" in German, the name among Galician Jews was an acronym for *zera tzadikim*, "descendant of the righteous," and was a tribute to the memory of distinguished and pious ancestors. Among Lithuanian Jews, however, Satz is the acronym referring to a cantor (*shaliah tzibbur*). What among other Jews was the name Schatz, or Shatz, was pronounced Satz by Lithuanian Jews.

SAVITZKY (G) From Sawicze, a town in Poland.

SCHACHTEL (O) or (H) House No. 99 in the Frankfurt ghetto had the sign of a *schachtel*, "band box." The Jewish family name is, however, a disguised form of *shohet*, the ritual slaughterer in the community.

SCHAFFER (D) Yiddish for "administrator." A name taken by a *gabbai*, a leader in the community.

SCHAFFNER (O) Schaffner is a steward or manager of a business or an estate.

SCHARF (D) Scharf or Sharfman means "sharp" and is a translation of the Hebrew *harif*, a term used to describe a brilliant student of the Talmud.

SCHARFSTEIN (O) Scharfstein means "sharpening stone" and may refer to a knife grinder, a butcher, or a ritual slaughterer.

SCHEIER (P) Scheier, Schayer, and Schauer are variations of Schorr, a symbolic reference to the name Joseph (Deuteronomy 33:17 compares Joseph to an ox—*shor*, in Hebrew).

SCHEINBERG (M) or (G) Although Scheinberg may be the Yiddish for the town of Schoenberg, in western Prussia, most people with this family name honored a matriarch called Shayna. Other variations of the name are Schein, Scheinman, Schenman, Schenberg, Schenberger, Scheinberger, Scheinfeld, Schenfeld.

SCHERTZER (G) "Jester," in German, but it really is derived from Siercza, a village in Galicia.

SCHICK (A) Schick, Shick, or Shik is either the acronym Sh*em* Y*israel* K*odesh*, "the name of Israel is holy," or it may be a name assumed by descendants of the famous sixteenth-century Italian rabbi, Sh*muel Yehudah* K*atzenellenbogen*.

SCHIMMEL (P) In German this word means either "a white horse" or "mildew," but the Jewish name has no connection with either. It is a diminutive of Shimon (Simon).

SCHINDLER (O) "Shingler," in German.

SCHINKEL (O) Schinkel, or Shenkel, means "a small inn or tavern." The owner of such a place adopted this name.

SCHLEIFER (O) *or* (G) "Knife grinder" or "diamond polisher," in German, or one who comes from Schleife, a town in Silesia.

SCHLOSS (O) One who made locks. See Schlossman.

SCHLOSSBERG (G) There are a number of communities throughout Germany called Schlossberg. They are places where there is a castle *(Schloss)* on the top of a hill *(Berg)*.

SCHLOSSMAN (O) In Yiddish *shlos* is "lock" and the name signifies either a locksmith or a dealer in locks or hardware.

SCHMELKIN (P) Schemlke is a variant of Schmulke, a diminutive of Shmuel (Samuel). Schmelkin is "a descendant of Samuel."

SCHMUKLER (O) From the Polish *Szmurklerz*, "braider," one who works with ornaments, with lace or braid for clothing. These items were in great demand because of the fashions of that generation, and Jews were very much involved in this work.

SCHNEEBALG (D) The word means "snowy figure" and was applied to a very old man as he appeared to the naming commission.

SCHNITMAN (O) *Schnittwäre* are "dry goods" in German and Schnitman is a dry goods merchant.

SCHOENTEIL (F) This was a name assumed by some Jewish

families in Germany in honor of Napoleon, who brought them freedom. Schoenteil is the German translation of Bonaparte.

SCHONBRUNN (G) A town in Moravia. The Jewish residents of this community and from other communities in Moravia and Bohemia were expelled by the Austrian empress Maria Theresa, and they found refuge in communities in Hungary across the border. Many later on preserved their places of origin in the family names they assumed.

SCHRAM (D) Schram, or Schramm, means "slight facial scar" and was probably the reason that this name was given to the bearer.

SCHRETER (O) Schreter means "cutter of cloth," the name taken by a tailor.

SCHRIFT (O) From Szrift, which means, in Polish, "printing type." The name taken by a printer, typesetter, or operator of a foundry.

SCHULSINGER (O) The German for "cantor."

SCHULTZ (D) From the German *Schultheiss*, "village magistrate," "overseer," the name taken by a synagogue official in a community.

SCHUPACK (O) Schupack means "pickerel" in Russian and signifies a dealer in fish. Another form of the name is Schupakevitch. In Polish there is a word *Szupak*, which means "sandpaper" and would indicate cabinet worker.

SCHWARTZBERG (G) The word means "black mountain," in German, and there is actually a Black Mountain in Poland.

SCHWEID (G) From the Polish *Szwed*, "Swede." This would indicate a person who came to Poland from areas in Germany occupied by the Swedes in the seventeenth century.

SCHWERSENSKY (G) From Schwersenz, a town in Posen.

SEILER (P) *and* (O) German for "rope maker," but Seiler became a symbolic word for Israel and contained the letters of that name. After it became an accepted patronymic for Israel, rope makers discarded it and began to use another name, Strikman.

SELDIS (M) Seldis, Seldes, Seldin is from Selde, a woman's name that means "good fortune," "blessing." Sedlis is a reversed form of that name. In Yiddish the name is more common as Zelda.

SELIG, SELIGMAN (P) Selig is the translation of Asher and means "happy" or "blessed." It is sometimes expanded to Seligman or Seligmann. Sometimes it is spelled with a "z" in place of the "s" and with a "k" in place of the "g," so that we get all kinds of combinations: Zelig, Zelik, Selik, etc.

SELTZER (O) A salt merchant or salt producer. This was a government monopoly and important people held that position.

SENELNICK (O) Senelnick, Sinilnik, or Senelick is the Russian for one in the dyeing trade who used the woad herb. For a long time the woad was the only source of blue vegetable dye in Europe, until it was finally replaced by indigo.

SERED (G) From Serenda, a town in Czechoslovakia.

SERTELS (M) Sertel is a nickname for Sarah.

SHABAD (A) For sh*aliah* b*et din* or sh*amash* b*et din,* a sort of bailiff of the rabbinic court.

SHAFRAN (O) *or* (D) Russian for "saffron," and the name would signify either a merchant who sold this spice or the one who had saffron-colored (red) hair.

SHAMES (O) The Hebrew for sexton.

SHANDALOV (O) Shandal is Polish for "shingle," and Shandalov would be "the son of the shingler," the equivalent of the German Schindler.

SHAPIRO (G) The city of Speyer in Rhenish Bavaria, Germany, has given us many name forms. The Jews first settled there at the end of the eleventh century and were compelled to leave in the middle of the fourteenth century. Large numbers of these Jews settled in Poland, Bohemia, Hungary, and Russia, and their name variants are: Shapiro, Spira, Spire, Spier, Spiro, Spero, Chapiro, Sprai, Szpir, Saphir, and Spear.

SHARF (D) "Sharp," in Yiddish is a translation of the Hebrew *harif*, a term used to describe a brilliant Talmudic student.

SHARLOTT (A) Stands for s*halom rav leohave toratekha*, "great is the peace for those who love your Torah" (Psalm 119:165).

SHATZKY (G) From Szacki, a town near Minsk in White Russia.

SHERER (O) Yiddish for "barber."

SHERESHEFSKY (G) From Szereszow, near Pruzany, in Russian Poland.

SHERMAN (O) A dealer in woolen cloth. Since the cloth had to be cut with shears *(Scher* or *Sher)*, this is how the name developed.

SHEVIN (M) A descendant of Sheva, short for Bat Sheva (Bathsheba).

SHIFRIN (M) Descendant of Shifra, a Biblical name.

SHIGON (G) From Szygany, a village in Russia.

SHLENSKY (G) Shlensky and Shlonsky are derived from the village of Szlazak, in Russian Poland.

SHNITKE (G) From Sznitki, a town in Lithuania.

SHOLK (O) *or* (D) Russian for "silk." The name was either assumed by a silk merchant or described a person who wore the material.

SHTULL (F) *Shtul* is Yiddish for "steel" and symbolizes the inner strength and faith of the Jew.

SHULRUF (O) From the Yiddish *Shulrufer*, one who calls people to services. A name for a sexton.

SIDELKO (O) Sidelko is Ukrainian for "awl" and was a worker in leather or a shoemaker.

SIEGEL (O) Siegel is the German for "seal." An engraver of seals would be called Siegel or Siegler. Jews were very prominent in the occupation of seal engraving in the eighteenth century. Other variations are Ziegler, Ziegelman, Ziegel, Siegelman. This name should not be confused with Segal which is an acronym for a Levite, although Segal and Siegel are often pronounced alike in English.

SILBERBERG (G) Silberberg, or Silverberg, is either a town in Silesia or a town in Poland.

SILBERMAN (O) Silberman, or Silverman, is a family name derived from the trade in silver.

SILVERMINTZ (O) Silvermintz may be a mint plant used in popular medicine by the village healer, or a silver coin, referring to one in the money-lending business.

SILVERSTEIN (O) Silverstein is "litharge" or "lead monoxide" and was a name assumed by a jeweler.

SIMKIN (P) Simkin means "son or descendant of Shimon (Simon)."

SIMONSKY (G) From Simony, the name of communities in Poland, Lithuania, and the Ukraine.

SIROTA (D) Sirota in Slavic means "orphan," and may describe one who actually was an orphan or one who looked sad and depressed.

SIVITZ (G) From Siwica, a town in White Russia.

SKLAR (O) Polish and Ukrainian for "glazier."

SKORA (O) Skora means "leather" in Polish, and the name would indicate one who dealt in hides or skins or leather.

SKUDIN (G) From Szkudy, a town in Lithuania.

SKURNIK (O) "One who tans leather," in Polish, or anyone in the leather trade.

SKYER (G) From Skiery, a village in Lithuania

SLADOVSKY (G) Sladovsky, or Shladovsky, from Sladow in Poland.

SLAVIN (M) Slavin, or Slovin, means "descended from Slawa," the Polish name that means "glory." In Yiddish this Polish word became Slava, Slova, Sluva, or Sliva.

SLEPIN (G) From Slepnia, near Minsk, White Russia.

SLONIMSKY (G) From Slonim, a town in Poland.

SLUTZKY (G) From Slutzk, a town in the province of Minsk, Russia.

SMILANSKY (G) From Smilanka, a town in Lithuania.

SMOLER (O) From the Ukrainian *smolyar*, "burner of tar," used to waterproof roofs and ships.

SMORGANSKY (G) From Smorgon, a town in Lithuania.

SOBOL (M) A popular name for women in Poland and Russia.

SOKOLOW (G) Sokolow, Sokoloff, Sokolowsky, Sokol, Sokolsky, all come from the word *sokol*, which in Polish and Russian means "falcon." The name is carried by hundreds of localities, large and small, because the word *sokol* came to denote "a hero."

SOLARZ (O) "Salt merchant," in Polish.

SOLODAR (O) Solodar is from the Russian *zolotar*, meaning "goldsmith."

SOLOVEICHIK (G) Although popularly derived from the Russian for "little nightingale," the name is actually derived from the village of Solwiez in the Grodno District of Poland—now Russia.

SOROKA (D) Soroka means "magpie" in Russian and was applied by the naming commission to a talkative person.

SOROTZKIN (G) From Serotzk, a town in the district of Lomza, Russian Poland.

SOURKES (M) Sourkes, Sirkes, Sirkin are all matronymics of Sarah, affectionately called Sorke, in Yiddish.

SPECTOR (O) Spector was the title of the inspector or supervisor of a school, but was a name often taken by an ordinary tutor (*melamed*) in the household of a rich Jew who had special permission to reside in the large cities of Russia where other Jews could not live.

SPEISHANDLER (O) From the German for "grocer," "a dealer in food." The name is often anglicized to Spicehandler, which changes the meaning somewhat.

SPERLING (D) German for "sparrow," a name given to a vivacious, active person.

SPETT (O) Spett is the old German for "rag." The name was taken by a rag dealer.

SPIEGLER (O) "Mirror maker," in German.

SPILKY (O) *Shpilke* is Yiddish for "pin," and the name was taken by a dealer in notions.

SPITZ (G) Spitz, or Spitzer, is from Spitz, a town in Austria.

SPIVAK (O) In the Slavic languages Spivak means "singer," especially one who sings in a religious service. This name was adopted by a cantor.

SPRINGER (D) A nickname for a person who was very vivacious.

SPRITZER (D) In German this means "sprinkler" or "one who spatters" and may refer to one who ejects spittle while talking. The name may have been given to someone who was actually doing this; or it may have been a derogatory name forced upon an individual by the naming officials.

SRULOFF (P) Sruloff, or Sroloff, is a descendant of Srol, Srul—short forms of Yisrael.

STAMPFER (G) From Stampfen, a town in Slovakia, formerly part of Hungary.

STAWITSKY (G) From Stawiszcze, a town in the Ukraine.

STEINBERG (G) There are many places by the name in Germany, and there is one town in Hungary. There is actually a Stone Mountain (*Steinberg*) near Brody, Galicia. Sometimes the name is taken from a place where there was a hill of stones.

STEINER (G) *or* (O) Steiner is often derived from any one of the many localities all over Poland which are called Kamien. The translation of *Kamien* is "stone" or "rock." Sometimes the presence of a rock formation caused a number of localities in Galicia to be called *shteyn* in Yiddish and their Jewish inhabitants were referred to as Steiner. But a number of the German Steiners took their name from the occupation of jewelers. Jewelers were often called Steiner because they dealt in precious stones, called *Edelsteine* in German.

STEINITZ (G) From Steinitz, a town in Moravia.

STELLMACHER (O) "Cartwright," in German, or a carriage maker or one who sold them.

STENDAL (G) From Stendal, a town in Magdeburg, Westphalia.

STERNIN (G) From the village of Sterniany in White Russia. Many Sternins became Stern.

STEUER (O) Steuer means "tax" or "duty" in German. The name was assumed by a collector of these.

STICKER (O) The German for a worker with gold braid and lacing.

STIER (P) Stier is the German translation of the Hebrew *shor* ("ox"), the *kinnui* for Joseph.

STOLLER (O) From the Ukrainian and Russian *stolyar*, "cabinet maker" or "carpenter."

STOLPER (G) From Stolpce, a town in White Russia, or from Stolp, in Pomerania.

STRAHL (P) Strahl means "ray" in German and is a translation of the Hebrew names Meir or Uri.

STRASHUN (G) From Streszyn, a village near Wilno.

STRIZOWER (G) From Strizov, a town in Galicia.

STROH (P) Shelomo (Solomon) was pronounced by some as Sloma. *Sloma* means "straw" in Polish, and when heard by the local officials, it was changed to Stroh, which means "straw" in German.

STROM (G) Strom is a German word meaning "stream," but this name is taken from the name of the village of Schrom, in Prussian Silesia.

STURM (G) Sturm has no connection with the German "storm." It is taken from the town of Szrem, near Posen, Poland. In Yiddish the town was called Strim and was often also pronounced Sturm.

SUKENIK (O) Sukenik is the Russian for "a dealer in cloth."

SULZ (G) The name of a community in Württemberg and in Alsace.

SULZBACH (G) A town in Bavaria.

SULZBERG (G) Sulzburg and Sulzberger are communities in Baden and Bavaria.

SUSSMAN (P) Sussman is a popular Jewish first name from the Middle Ages and it means "sweet man." Its popularity is attested by the fact that it became a byname for the Hebrew names Eliezer, Yoel (Joel), Meshulam, and Azriel.

SVIRSKY (G) From Svir, a town near Kovno, Lithuania.

TABACHIN (O) *and* (P) *Tabach* means "butcher" or "cook" (from the Hebrew *tabah*). Tabachin means "the son of a butcher or a cook."

TABACHNIK (O) The Polish and Russian word for seller or manufacturer of snuff.

TADLIS (P) Tadl is an affectionate form which means "little David" and Tadlis means "descendant of David."

TALESNICK (O) Talesnick, Talisnick, or Talisman refers to one who sells or makes prayer shawls.

TALMACH (O) Tolmach is the Russian adaptation of the German *Dolmetsch*, "interpreter." One form of the name is Talmach which is often anglicized to Talmadge.

TAMARKIN (M) Tamara is a woman's name that was popular among Russian Jews. Tamarkin indicates a descendant of Tamar or Tamara.

TAMBOR (O) "Drummer," in Yiddish.

TANZER (D) This is the German-Yiddish for "dancer." Some individuals achieved the distinction of being very adept at dancing, especially at community weddings.

TARADASH (F) In appearance, this name resembles the word *taradaj* which in Slavic means "talkative old woman." Actually, this is a disguised form for *Torah Dat,* "Torah law."

TARGOWNIK (O) "Merchant," "market man," in Polish.

TARLER (G) *or* (O) Either from Tarlo, a town in the province of Lublin, Poland, or from *tarlo,* which in Polish means "file," "grater," and would refer to a seller of hardware.

TARSHISH (P) *or* (F) *or* (O) In the book of Jonah we are told that the prophet tried to escape in a ship bound for Tarshish. This association may have caused the name to be selected by a person called Jonah. A second possibility is that Tarshish is a precious stone mentioned in the Bible and may have been selected just as the product of one's imagination or, perhaps, by a dealer in gems.

TARTAKOVER (G) From Tartak, a town in Poland.

TAUB (P) *or* (H) While some German-Jewish families derived their name from the house bearing the sign of the *Taube* ("dove"), most names which have the element Taub are patronymics for Jonah (which in Hebrew is "dove").

TAXIN (O) Taxin, or Taksen, was the one who levied the government taxes on various items such as meat, milk, bread, salt, etc.

TCHERIKOVER (G) From Tcherikov, a town in the province of Mohilev, Russia.

TEIG (O) Teig means "dough" in German, and Teig and Teigman are names taken by a baker.

TEITELBAUM (F) This name is based upon Psalm 92:12, which states, "the righteous shall flourish like the palm tree." *Teitelbaum* is "date palm," in German. Others selected their name from the second half of the verse "they shall grow like a cedar in Lebanon" and took the name *Zederbaum* ("cedar tree"). Since our forefathers were not expert in botany, some also selected *Tannenbaum* ("fir tree") as a reference to this verse.

TELLER (O) Teller is the dish which identified the barber-surgeon in eastern Europe (like the striped pole in front of the present-day barber shop). This name was taken by a barber-surgeon.

TEMKIN (M) From Tema, which is an abbreviated form of Tamar or Tamara.

TENDLER (O) Tendler, or Tandler, denotes a dealer in secondhand furniture or clothes. It is a name especially found among Austrian and Galician Jews.

TEOMIM (P) *or* (F) Teomim, or Tomim, is the Hebrew name for the zodiac sign Gemini. Children born during that period of the calendar were given the name Teomim (which is also the source of the English name Thomas). From a personal name it became a family name. Sometimes a person born during that time selected the name as a family name because the zodiac sign is called in Hebrew *mazal* and the selection was a hope for good luck.

TEPLITZ (G) Teplitz or Teplitzky are from Tepliczka, a famous resort town in Czechoslovakia.

TESSLER (O) Ukrainian for "carpenter."

TICKTIN (G) From the Yiddish for Tykocin, a town in Poland. Tykocin is also a Jewish family name.

TISCHLER (O) Tischler, or Tishler, is a carpenter or cabinet maker.

TOBIAS (P) Tobias is another form of the Hebrew name Tuvia. More often it would be translated into the German Gutman or Goodman.

TOPOREK (O) *Topor* is the Polish word for "axe," and Toporek means "little axe." The name was assumed either by a carpenter or a butcher.

TRAININ (M) From Treinel, Trandel, Trana, Treine—all Jewish developments of the German woman's name Terine, originally from the French name Estérine.

TRATTNER (G) From Tratna, a town in Galicia.

TRILLING (G) Trilling, Trillinger, and Tringler are names derived from Wassertruedingen, a town in Franconia, Bavaria.

TROCK (G) From Troki, a town in Lithuania.

TRUBNICK (O) "Chimney sweep," in Yiddish.

TUCHMAN (O) The Yiddish for "cloth merchant."

TULMAN (O) From the German *Tull*, "lace." A milliner or dressmaker.

TUNIK (G) From a town near Minsk.

TURBIN (G) From Turbin, a town in Poland.

TURETZKY (G) Turetz and Turetzky are from Turetz, a town near Minsk, in White Russia.

TUROFF (G) Turoff, Turov, Turofsky, Turover are from Turov in White Russia.

TUROWITZ (G) From Turowicze, a town in Poland.

TWERSKY (F) *or* (G) Menahem Nahum of Chernobyl (died 1798) was the founder of an important dynasty of Hasidim. He took Twersky as his family name, because a mystic tradition states that the Messiah will make his first appearance in Tiberias, one of the four holy cities in Palestine. Twersky means "one coming from Tveriah" (the Hebrew name for Tiberias). There is also a town called Tver in Russia, and many who carry the name Twersky may have originated from that place.

TYGEL (O) Tygel is a Polish word which means "crucible." The crucible was very important in the work of the goldsmith, and the artisan selected this as a family name. Other names for a goldsmith are Zlotnick and Zolotar.

ULMAN (G) Ulman and Ulmann are from Ulm, a town in Württemberg, Germany.

UNGAR (G) Ungar, or Unger, is "Hungarian," in German.

UNNA (G) From Unna in the duchy of Berg, Germany.

VARON (P) Varon is a Sephardic name. In Spanish the word means "man" and is a reference to Moses, who was called *Varon de Dios,* "the man of God."

del VECCHIO (D) The oldest Italian Jewish families traced their descent from a number of families who had been brought to Rome by Titus after the destruction of Jerusalem and who remained there. These families are, in Italian, Rossi ("reds"), Adolescenti ("youths"), Pomis ("apples"), and Anav ("humble," in Hebrew). (The Anav families took on Italian versions of their names, Pietosi and Piatelli.) Another old family was named Bethel in Hebrew, which was translated to the Italian Casadio ("house of God") and Degli Mansi ("of the house") and De Synagoga *(bet hakneset,* in Hebrew). However, there was one family that traced its descent to Jews who were in Rome *before* Titus, and these called themselves del Vecchio, which means "old-timers" in distinction from the newcomers.

VELIKOFF (P) Velikoff, Velikov, or Velikovsky all contain the meaning "great one," a Russian translation of the Hebrew name Gedaliah.

VERBIN (G) Verbin, Werbin, Werben from Werbin, a town in the area of Volhynia, Russia.

VIGODA (O) Vigoda, Wygoda mean "inn" or "tavern," in Polish. There were hundreds of such places all over Poland and Jews were almost always in charge of them. Other names derived from this occupation are Wigodar, Wigodney.

VITKIN (M) Vita, or Wita, is a translation of Hayah, meaning "life" in Hebrew. Vitkin or Witkin mean "descended from Hayah."

WACHTEL (F) *or* (H) Wachtel means "quail" in German and may refer to one who lived near a place with a sign of the quail. However, it may be a name that was selected by a Jew who recalled God's mercy and providence in providing quail to the Israelites in their march through the wilderness.

WAGNER (O) This is the German word for a cartwright and would signify either one who makes wagons or coaches or one who is a driver of wagons or coaches.

WALKER (O) A fuller of woolen cloth. (The name is pronounced Val-ker.)

WALLERSTEIN (G) A town in Bavaria.

WANK (G) From Wankowa, a town in Galicia.

WAPNER (O) From *Wapno,* "quicklime." A dealer in lime.

WARBURG (G) A town in Westphalia, Germany.

WARNIK (O) Ukrainian for "operator of salt works."

WARTEL (G) From Wartele, a village near Suwalki, Poland.

WASSERMAN (F) *or* (O) Either from the zodiac sign Aquarius, which would make it another *mazal* ("luck") name or from the occupation of "water carrier."

WAXMAN (O) From the German *Wachsman,* "a dealer in wax." Wax was sold in blocks, *Wachsstein,* and from here we get Waxstein, also a name for a wax dealer.

WECKER (O) A baker of white rolls *(Wecken* are white rolls in German).

WEIL (G) From Weil, a town in Württemberg, Germany. The name goes back to the end of the fourteenth century. Other forms are Weill, Weile, Weiler.

WEIN (O) A wine merchant. Sometimes the name has nothing to do with wine but is another spelling for Fein, "fine."

WEINBERG (G) In West Europe Weinberg indicates a mountain in Westphalia. East European Weinbergs derive their name from Wyntbark, a suburb of Danzig, where most of the Jewish population was concentrated. The Weinbergs of central Europe derive their name from the village of Weinberg, near Nikolsburg, Moravia.

WEINER (O) The Yiddish for "winemaker" or "wine dealer."

WEINGLASS (O) A wine shop had a picture of a vintage festival scene—*Weinlese* (in Yiddish, *Weinles*)—on the door or sign before it. After a while the meaning of *Weinles* was forgotten and Weinglass replaced it. The name was taken by the owner of a wine shop.

WEINLAUB (O) This was the vine garland which decorated a wine shop.

WEINREB (P) *or* (O) Weinreb means "vine" in German, and Weinraub is the Yiddish version of it. Weinstock is also a vine garland which decorated a wine shop. All these names were used by owners of wine shops. However, the word for vine became a symbol for the name Israel. When Joseph II issued the law compelling the Austrian Jews to assume family names, the officials forbade them from taking Hebrew names. But the Jews evaded the restriction by preserving a Hebrew name in a symbolic way. In Jeremiah 6:9 Israel is compared to a vine, and the above names reflect the prophet's words.

WEINSTEIN (O) Weinstein is the German for tartar that settles in the wine casks. It was very often selected as the family name by a dealer in wine.

WEISEL (G) The name originated in the town of Wesel in western Germany but spread into many communities all over Europe.

WERTHEIM (G) Wertheim and Wertheimer from Wertheim, a town in Hesse.

WETZLAR (G) A town in Germany.

WIEDER (F) From *Widder* which is the German for Ram or Aries, the sign of the zodiac. It was either assumed by a person born during that time or because of its association with the word *mazal*, which means luck, and the sign of the zodiac in Hebrew.

WINDNER (G) From Winden, the name of several places in Germany.

WINKLER (D) The owner of a shop located at a corner (*Winkel*, in German) was called Winkler.

WINNICK (O) A maker of brandy. "Distiller," in Russian.

WINOKUR (O) "Distiller," in Polish and Ukrainian.

WITTENBERG (G) A town in Germany.

WOLFBERG (P) This is one of the many disguised forms for the name Wolff, which is the *kinnui* for Benjamin. Other forms are Wolfenberg, Wolfsfeld, Wolfheim, Wolfsheimer, Wolfenstein, Wolfenthal, Wolfshaut, Wolfinger, Wolfenfeld.

WOLFISH (P) Wolfish or Walfisch, which mean "whale," is the *kinnui* for Ephraim, whose descendants were to multiply like fish.

WOLLMAN (O) "Trader in wool," in German.

WOLPER (P) The *kinnui* of Benjamin is Wolf or Wolfe, which was extended to Wolper.

WOSKOBOINIK (O) The Ukrainian word for "wax maker."

YAMPOL (G) From the town of Yampol (Jampol) in Podolia, Russia. Another form of the name is Yampolsky.

YANKELOWITZ (P) Yaakov (Jacob) popularly became Yankel. Yankelowitz means "son of Jacob."

YARMAK (A) An acronym for *yehe raavo min kodomoh,* "may it be Thy will." This was selected as a prayer by the person assuming the new name.

YATKEMAN (O) *Yatke* is Yiddish for "slaughterhouse," and Yatkeman is a butcher.

YAVETZ (F) *or* (A) In 1 Chronicles 4:9 there is a man by this name and in 1 Chronicles 2:55 there is a place by that name. But the name was really made famous by Rabbi Jacob Emden who called himself Yavetz by creating the acronym *Yaakov Emden ben Tzvi.* Since then a number of Jewish families adopted this name. It appears also as Yavitz and Javitz.

YISHTABACH (F) This is the name of one of the prayers in the

Siddur and was selected by a number of Ukrainian Jewish families.

YOLLES (P) From the Hebrew Yoel (Joel) we get Yolles, Yale, Yolleck, and Yule. Disguised forms are Yoelsdorf, Yoelberg, and Yollenberg and Yoelson.

ZACKHEIM (A) Although there is a community in Prussia by the name of Sackheim, the Jewish family name Zackheim is an acronym for *zak hem* which stands for *zera kodesh hem*, "they are the children of holy seed," symbolic of the descendants of martyrs.

ZAGER (G) From Zagory, a town in Lithuania.

ZAITZ (D) Zaitz, Zeitz are associated with Zaichik which means "little hare" and describes a lively person.

ZARCHIN (P) A descendant of Zorach.

ZARETSKY (G) Zaretsky is from *zariecze*, in Polish, which means "beyond the river." This was more specifically applied to the city of Shklov. There were two localities by that name, one on the Dnieper and the other "beyond the river."

ZASLAVSKY (G) From Zaslav, Saslavl, a town in Volhynia, Russia.

ZECKENDORF (G) A town near Bamberg, Bavaria.

ZEGMAN (O) Literally, "saw-man," a carpenter.

ZEIDNER (O) Zeidner, Seidner, Zeideman, Seidman, are all associated with the occupation of silk merchant. *Seide* is German for "silk."

ZEITLIN (M) Zeitel or Zertel are nicknames for Sarah or Tzipporah.

ZEITMAN (O) Literally, "time-man," but it refers to a watchmaker or clock seller.

ZELDA (M) Zelda, Selda, Selde, Zeldin, and Seldin are all from the woman's name Salida which means "happiness."

ZELEZNIKOV (O) "Dealer in iron," in Polish.

ZELIKOVITZ (P) Zelik (Zelig) is a translation of the Hebrew name Asher which means "happy" or "blessed." Zelikovitz means "descendant of Zelik." There are a number of ways in which the name Zelik was disguised as a family name: Zeligsberg, Zeligsheim, Zeligstein, Zeliger, Zelinger, Zelighaus. Asher was also disguised as a family name in the following forms: Ashburg, Aschenheim, Aschheim, Ashner, Aschenheimer, Ashman, Ashendorf.

ZEROBNICK (O) From *zarobnik*, the Polish for "day laborer."

ZEVIN (P) A descendant of Zev which is the Hebrew for Wolf which is the *kinnui* for Benjamin.

Z'FANSKY (F) Rabbi Samuel of Borodianka (near Kiev), a disciple of Menahem Nahum of Chernobyl, selected Z'fansky as his family name. There is a tradition among his followers that his choice was also to honor the city of Tiberias, but since Twersky was already a name selected by his master, he selected Safed, another of the four holy cities of the Holy Land. Z'fansky means "one coming from Safed." Other variations of this name are Sefansky, Zfass, Zfassman.

ZIMBALIST (O) The Germanic for one who plays the cymbals.

ZIMMERMAN (O) "Carpenter," in German.

ZIPPERSTEIN (M) Zipper stands for Tzipporah and the *-stein* was merely added as an embellishment.

ZITNIK (O) "Grain merchant," in Russian.

ZLATKIN (M) Zlate is the Slavic form of Golde. Zlatkin or Zlotkin is the equivalent of Goldes.

ZOREF (O) Zoref, or Soref, is the Hebrew for "goldsmith."

ZUCKERMAN (O) Literally, "sugar man." A confectioner or pastry maker.

ZUNDER (O) The German for "tinder." Before the invention of matches, tinder was used for kindling fire. A seller of tinder.

ZUNZ (G) From Zons, a town on the Rhine.

ZUPNICK (O) From the Polish word for the government official who was in charge of a salt mine.

ZWIEBEL (O) Zwiebel is the German for "onion," and the names Zwiebel, Zwibel, and Swibel indicated a green grocer.

ZWILLENBERG (G) Zwillenberg is the Yiddish for Zillenberg, a town in Upper Bavaria.

ZWIRN (O) Zwirn is the German word for "thread." The name was taken by a tailor.

Bibliography

DIETZ, ALEXANDER. *Stammbuch der frankfurter Juden.* Frankfurt am Main, 1907.

DREIFUSS, ERWIN MANUEL. *Die Familiennamen der Juden.* Frankfurt am Main, 1927.

DUKKES, YEHEZKEL. *Sefer Hakhmay Altona, Hamburg, Wandsbek.* Hamburg, 1905.

ESHEL, MOSHE HANINA. *Shemot Hamishpahah BeYisrael.* Haifa, 1967.

GRAY, G. BUCHANAN. *Studies in Hebrew Proper Names.* London, 1896.

GUMPERTZ, YEHIEL GEDALYA. "Kriat Shemot BeYisrael," *Tarbiz,* 1956.

HERSHBERG, A. S. "Shemot Ha-etzem Hapratiyim Haivriyim Batkufot Hakdumot," *Hatekufah,* XXII, XXV.

HORWITZ, MORDECAI HALEVI. *Avne Zikaron.* Frankfurt am Main, 1901.

KAGANOFF, BENZION C. "Jewish First Names through the Ages," *Commentary,* November, 1955.

———. "Jewish Surnames through the Ages," *Commentary,* September, 1956.

KESSLER, GERHARD. *Die Familiennamen der Juden in Deutschland.* Leipzig, 1935.

KOLATCH, ALFRED J. *These Are the Names.* New York, 1948.

KOSOVER, MORDECAI. "Shinui Hashemot Bimdinat Yisrael," *Bitzaron*, Nos. 149, 150, 151, 157, 159; 1952.

KUGELMASS, J. ALVIN. "Name-Changing—and What It Gets You." *Commentary*, August, 1952.

LAUTERBACH, JACOB Z. "The Naming of Children in Jewish Folklore, Ritual, and Practice," *CCAR Yearbook*, 42, 1932.

MAASS, ERNEST. "Integration and Name Changing among Jewish Refugees from Central Europe in the United States," *Names*, Journal of the American Name Society, Volume 6, No. 3 (September, 1958).

MAHLER, RAPHAEL. "Shemot Yehudiyim Shel Mekomot Bepolin Hayeshono," *Reshumot*, V, 1953.

NOTH, MARTIN. *Die israelitischen Personennamen im Rahmen der gemeinsemitischen Namengebung*. Hildesheim, 1966.

Oxford Dictionary of English Christian Names. 1947 Edition.

PEARLROTH, N. "Your Name," *Jewish Post and Opinion*.

PINE, L. G. *The Story of Surnames*. 1965

RABINOWITZ, ELIEZER SHELOMO. "Kinnuyay Mishpahah Ivriyim," *Reshumot*, V, VI, 1953.

SMITH, ELSDON C. *Treasury of Name Lore*. New York, 1967.

TALPIMON, S. *Kaytzad Livhor Shem Ivri*. Tel Aviv, 1949.

TKATZ, DUBER. *Kuntras Hashemot* (6 Vols.). Tel Aviv, 1955.

TRACHTENBERG, JOSHUA. *Jewish Magic and Superstition*. New York, 1939.

Yeda-Am, Journal of the Israel Folklore Society.

ZUNZ, LEOPOLD. *Die Namen der Juden*. Leipzig, 1837.

Index of Names

Index of Subjects